Hallelujah Kids

Resource for Moms - Recipes for Kids

Acknowledgments

Thank you Father God for my children and entrusting their care to me. Thanks Olin for the beautifully written foreword to this book and the work you did on your book *Pregnancy Children & The Hallelujah Diet*. Thank you Rev. Malkmus and Rhonda for your dedication to our health message. Thank you Linda, Judy, Paul and Jim for working with me on yet another big project. Thanks Mom for your continued support and being my partner in ministry. Thank you Candy for taking over full leadership of our homeschool group freeing me up to do this work. Thank you Bob for supporting the dietary choices I have made for our children and thanks boys for going along with me!

Foreword

When I first met Julie nearly four years ago, it was quite obvious that she was a vivacious and compassionate young lady. But, little did I realize what a tremendous blessing she would soon become as she fully embraced The Hallelujah Diet & Lifestyle℠, regained her health, and began ministering to the needs of others.

She has taken an active role in not only educating her children academically but also in providing them a spiritual and nutritional foundation they will carry with them the rest of their lives. She draws on her personal research, experience with her own children, and correspondence with an untold multitude of struggling parents to bring to you an invaluable resource in *Hallelujah Kids*.

Throughout the past nearly ten years, I've talked to hundreds of parents who knew they needed to take responsibility not only of their own health but that of their entire family. They struggled with how to implement a predominately raw plant-based diet with their children. They were unclear as to how to best nourish their children to enable them to stay slim and healthy, strengthen their immune system, and reduce their risk of sickness and chronic disease later in life.

Now, with *Hallelujah Kids*, parents can be empowered with a fundamental understanding of basic and simple nutritional principles based upon biblical principles as found in Genesis 1:29 that will enable them to equip their children with good dietary habits they will take with them throughout life. Their children will be nourished in a manner that allows for not only excellent physical development but also for optimal mental development and achievement. Healthy eating will become second nature – a new way of life they will not want to give up.

You will learn how to deal with those challenging situations, peer pressure, school lunches, and special events as your children become an example of optimal health and physical and mental fitness. As you set the example, your family will become a powerful witness to the power of living foods.

One of the major challenges parents are initially faced with is what to feed their children that will encourage them to transition over to a healthy diet and lifestyle. *Hallelujah Kids* provides a wealth of recipes for all occasions that will please the palate of even the pickiest eaters. Through the testimonies of others, you will share in the challenges others have faced and the victories they have won.

Julie has put together more than a book. This is a resource manual you will value for years to come.

Olin Idol, N.D., C.N.C.
V/P Health Hallelujah Acres®
Author of *Pregnancy, Children, and The Hallelujah Diet*

Table Of Contents

Introduction

Since publishing *Thank God for Raw* and *Healthy 4 Him* about my personal experience with The Hallelujah Diet & Lifestyle℠, I have corresponded with thousands of parents who, besides wanting to adopt this way of life for themselves, want to teach it to their children. *Hallelujah Kids* is a culmination of ideas, recipes and tips from parents who have made positive changes in their families' diets and lifestyles. The purpose of this book is to show you that kids can eat healthfully! Many do enjoy living a healthy lifestyle. I should include a disclaimer here—we do not claim that our children adhere perfectly to The Hallelujah Diet® or have perfect health. There has only been one perfect person on this planet! We do not want to place our kids in a position of having to meet others' expectations. We simply want to add to your knowledge base some stories, suggestions, recipes, and food facts that will help you in your quest for good health.

The greatest things I can teach my kids, after loving God with all their hearts and loving others, is to take wonderful care of their body temples.

"Know ye not that ye are the temple of God, and that the spirit of God dwelleth in you? If any man defile the temple of God, him shall God destroy for the temple of God is holy, which temple ye are."

1 Corinthians 3:16-17

It is awesome that you are interested in helping your families be healthier! Getting them to participate may be a bit of a challenge and will involve patience, compromise, and possibly even some tears. But it will be well worth all your efforts. Not every child will react in the same way to the proposed dietary and lifestyle changes. Some may verbally rebel and others may go on a hunger strike. Some may sneak food while others will love carrot juice. Some will hate eating "leaves" as my younger son used to say and others will come up with their own creations to put on them. Some will eat spinach but not Brussels sprouts. Some will need to learn self-discipline, some will want to study and learn, and some might even take over the kitchen!

Let's take a look now at many thought-provoking and helpful ideas. I hope that these will spur you on toward the goal of abundant life that God wants for you. I wish you and your kids the very best of health.

The Hallelujah Diet®?

In short, The Hallelujah Diet® is a natural plant-based diet as described in Genesis 1:29...

And God said, "Behold I have given you every herb bearing seed, which is upon the face of all the earth, and every tree, in which is the fruit of a tree yielding seed; to you it shall be for meat."

Genesis 1:29

You will find details on pages 29 and 31.

Why The Hallelujah Diet®?

The answer to this question may best be answered by some astonishing facts that will leave you asking, Why NOT The Hallelujah Diet®?

"Autopsies performed on children six years of age and older who (died) in accidents have shown that the majority exhibit fatty streaks on their arteries along with some narrowing of the coronary arteries."
Dr. Jay Gordon www.drjgordon.com

Fatty streaks in their arteries, those little blood vessels that go to their sweet little hearts?

Dr. David Katz of the Yale University School of Medicine says that "children in the United States and Canada are the first cohort in modern memory looking at a shorter life expectancy than their parents because of epidemic obesity and diabetes."

Approximately 30.3 percent of children (ages 6 to 11) are overweight and 15.3 percent are obese. For adolescents (ages 12 to 19), 30.4 percent are overweight and 15.5 percent are obese.

Excess weight in childhood and adolescence has been found to predict overweight in adults.

Type 2 diabetes in children and adolescents has increased dramatically in a short period. The parallel increase of obesity in children and adolescents is reported to be the most significant factor for the rise in diabetes.

Persistently elevated blood pressure levels have been found to occur about 9 times more frequently among obese children and adolescents (ages 5 to 18) than in non-obese.

Among growing youth, bone and cartilage in the process of development are not strong enough to bear excess weight. As a result, a variety of orthopedic complications occur in children and adolescents with obesity. In young children, excess weight can lead to bowing and overgrowth of leg bones.

American Obesity Association (AOA) www.obesity.org

In 2004, approximately 12,500 children and adolescents younger than 21 will be diagnosed with cancer in the United States. Of the 2,800 children who will die of the disease, nearly one third will die from leukemia.

People Living with Cancer www.plwc.org

I want healthy, vibrant, life-loving kids and I'll bet you do too! I can honestly say that adding an abundance of fresh fruits and vegetables to my boys' menus has kept them out of the doctor's office for nearly six years! No antibiotics, no shots, no drugs, no BILLS! (We did have to deal with dog bites and broken ankles, all of which healed quickly and completely.)

"I will praise thee; for I am fearfully and wonderfully made: marvelous are thy works; and that my soul knoweth right well."

Psalm 139:14

Up to 20 percent of children have some degree of asthma. For many children their asthma will reoccur when they are adults. Asthma diagnosed as mild will, in some children, develop into severe asthma. Asthma is one of the most common diseases in the world and it is increasing dramatically. There is currently no cure for asthma. Most people with asthma are "managed" by medication and by avoiding triggers.

www.childhoodasthma.com

Hallelujah Kids

Asthma and Cancer gone...

We are new Health Ministers since Nov 03 und are 2 Years on the Hallelujah Diet & Lifestyle. We started cold turkey because of my husband's fresh diagnosis with Prostate cancer. We have four kids, now 5, 8, 11 and 14 years and one baby on the way.

We started all four kids on 1 serving of barley grass powder and one 8 oz. glass of carrot juice in the morning, first with apple. We changed from white noodles, rice and bread to wheat and little by little with a small dinner plate salad, mainly spinach. They all love avocado and fruits of all kinds so I make sure we have plenty in the house. I bake my own bread out of spelt or whole wheat, with lots of different grains in it. For breakfast we eat organic rolled oats with warm water with soaked nuts, millet, flaxseed, honey and different berries or banana in it. I love it myself since I'm pregnant. On the side I fix a big fruit bowl. The 2 older kids take turns every morning to juice for all of us, so the work is more divided.

My oldest son's asthma has cleared up completely. The kids haven't been to the doctor in 2 years. My husband is cancer free now! We don't go out and eat that often anymore because food tastes better at home. The kids play outside in any weather (with the proper clothes), bike, swim etc. I'm so proud of them. Our new family addition will be completely raised on the Hallelujah Diet.

from Roy and Ursula P.
Lubbock Texas

Are you feeding your kids food or fodder?

People ask me all the time how in the world I get my kids to eat fruits and vegetables. Well, let me tell you it's been interesting. God opened my eyes through the materials published by Rev. Malkmus of Hallelujah Acres®. The boys and I studied together and continue to do so.

We learned
    that God created us with truly miraculous self-healing bodies;
    that carrots make juice;
    that we are called to present our whole selves as living sacrifices to God;
    that meat consumption is linked to higher cancer rates;
    that God established natural laws;
    that kohlrabi is food;
    that exercise can and should be fun;
    that there really is a way to be healthy!

Unfortunately, challenges are everywhere so the children need to understand why you will no longer be buying and eating certain "foods."

A study of children in 40 countries found that the incidence of juvenile diabetes was directly related to diet: The higher the consumption of cow's milk and other animal products, the greater the chance of developing diabetes. Conversely, children who consumed a largely vegetarian diet had a much lower incidence of diabetes.
The American Journal of Nutrition, 2000, pp1525-1529

The first step in educating ourselves about what we were eating was to make lists of all the "foods" we could think of. Then we looked up, in every source we could find, the definition of the word food. Next we compared each "food" on our lists to the definitions of food. Not many of them qualified. Try it!

Hallelujah Kids

Webster's definitions of food:
1: material consisting essentially of protein, carbohydrate, and fat used in the body of an organism to sustain growth, repair, and vital processes and to furnish energy; *also*: such food together with supplementary substances (as minerals, vitamins)
2: nutriment in solid form
3: something that nourishes, sustains, or supplies

Let's see: French fries? Very few vitamins and minerals there. Candy? No growth sustaining going on. Soda pop? Nourishing-not!

Webster's definitions of fodder:
1 : something fed to domestic animals; *especially* : coarse food for cattle, horses, or sheep
2 : inferior or readily available material used to supply a heavy demand

---

They also had to learn to read labels. Talk about a science lesson!

We discovered that "foods" requiring a label usually aren't food! One time we were standing in line at the grocery store. The boys spotted a new flavor of nacho chips and wanted them. So I told them I'd buy them if they could read the label for me and tell me what exactly it was they wanted to eat. They got started right away but didn't get too far! A few seconds later, they put the bag back on the shelf, hung their heads and said, "Ok, Mom, we get it." The ladies behind us in line removed a few items from their carts as well!

Actual label from an unidentified bag of corn chips...

Ingredients: Corn, Vegetable Oil (Contains One or More of the Following: Corn, Soybean, or Sunflower Oil), Maltodextrin, Salt, Cheddar Cheese (Cultured Milk, Salt, Enzymes), Parmesan Cheese (Cultured Milk, Salt, Enzymes), American Cheese (Cultured Milk, Salt, Enzymes), Swiss Cheese (Cultured Milk, Salt, Enzymes), Colby Cheese (Cultured Milk, Salt, Enzymes), Whey, Dried Cream, Partially Hydrogenated Soybean Oil, Buttermilk, Monosodium Glutamate, Onion Powder, Tomato Powder,

Disodium Phosphate, Artificial Colors (Including Yellow 6 Lake, Yellow 5, Yellow 6, Blue 1, Red 40, Turmeric), Citric Acid, Natural and Artificial Flavors, Sodium Diacetate, Nonfat Milk, Garlic Powder, Butter (Cream and Salt), Whey Protein Concentrate, Lactic Acid, Corn Starch, Sour Cream (Cultured Cream, Nonfat Milk), Yeast Extract, Glycerol, and Gum Arabic.

What do you think? Food or Fodder?

Besides all the crazy sounding artificial ingredients in this package notice all the dairy products.

> A study published in the American Journal of Clinical Nutrition in June, 1993, confirmed that there is a definite correlation between cow's milk and the incidence of diabetes.
> "You will never see an advertisement with a famous movie star proudly wearing a white mustache, properly labeled as containing 300,000 white blood cells and 25,000 bacteria."
> Dr. John McDougall

Another important lesson to teach your kids is what different fruits and veggies are good for. Carrots are good for our eyes, for example. They contain beta carotene, which can reduce the chance of eye diseases like macular degeneration.

Spinach may be good mood food. It contains lots of folic acid. If your body doesn't have enough folic acid, you may feel depressed.

Blueberries have antioxidants which help neutralize harmful by-products of metabolism called "free radicals" that can lead to cancer and other age-related diseases. "So," Ryan says, "if we don't want cancer, it sounds like eating fresh blueberries is a good idea!" You got it, buddy!

Honestly though, I can't tell you how many meals I made that my sons would not eat. I found myself in tears many nights. Then one night my mom asked, "Who's the mother over there?" I decided it was time to withhold altogether the foods I didn't want them eating and start replacing them with God's natural foods (they were not used to them yet but they quickly discovered how wonderful they are!).

Sometimes kids will eat good food if we expose them to it in a way that makes them curious rather than give it to them and tell them to eat it. Once my mom asked me to pick up a loaf of bread from a local bakery for her and bring it to church on Sunday.

Hallelujah Kids

After carrying this loaf of bread through church from hour to hour, I concluded that my mom wasn't there. So I brought the bread into my classroom and sat it on the desk with my purse. A little while later, one of the children asked me what was in the bag. I told her it was bread from a baker who grinds his own wheat and makes delicious bread. I then offered her a taste. Well, she loved it and the other kids wanted to know what they were missing out on. So I tore off a big hunk and pinched off pieces for them. They ate half the loaf! When class was over, my son Corbin walked in and said, "Grandma wants me to bring her bread to her." Oops!

There were a few nights my kids went to bed hungry. I learned that I had to make some compromises. I do occasionally compromise with some of the "vegan junk foods." Even so, they learned that Mom meant business. It was a battle of wills for awhile. For some reason I thought they would actually starve themselves to death and I would be responsible. I could see the headlines: *Mom Convicted for Withholding Hot Dogs and Chicken Nuggets. Lack of Pizza Contributes to Starvation of Two Young Boys. Evil Mother Forces Children to Drink Water instead of Soda!*

Once we were over that nasty hump, we discovered many foods that they actually enjoyed! We made a deal that they at least have to taste a new food. If they don't like it, it doesn't come back by popular demand—unless, of course, I like it in which case I make it for myself!

Why Not Soda Pop?

Drinking soda helped to destroy my health. I was so addicted to colas that I would walk to the gas station late at night for a fix. As a teenager, I would drink cola for breakfast! Coming off these sodas was the hardest part of my transition to The Hallelujah Diet®. I am very thankful my kids don't like the bubbles!

Soft drinks contain high levels of phosphates that contribute to high levels of blood phosphates. When phosphates are high and calcium levels are low in the blood, the body pulls calcium out of the bones. Thus soft drinks may be a major contributor to poor bone and teeth development in children, as well as osteoporosis in later years. There is no place in the diet for soft drinks for those desirous of optimal health. They should NEVER be introduced to children.

Olin Idol, *Pregnancy, Children & The Hallelujah Diet*, page 57

Reporting in *The Lancet*, a British medical journal, a team of Harvard researchers presented the first evidence linking soft drink consumption to childhood obesity. They found that 12-year-olds who drank soft drinks regularly were more likely to be overweight than those who didn't. For each additional daily serving of sugar-sweetened soft drink consumed during the nearly two-year study, the risk of obesity increased 1.6 times.

Sugar isn't the only ingredient in soft drinks that causes tooth problems. The acids in soda pop are also notorious for etching tooth enamel in ways that can lead to cavities. "Acid begins to dissolve tooth enamel in only 20 minutes," notes the *Ohio Dental Association*.

A 1994 Harvard study of bone fractures in teenage athletes found a strong association between cola beverage consumption and bone fractures in 14-year-old girls. The girls who drank cola were about five times more likely to suffer bone fractures than girls who didn't consume soda pop.

Pediatrics Academy Calls for Elimination of Soda in Schools

By THE ASSOCIATED PRESS

CHICAGO, Jan. 4, 2004 (AP) - Soft drinks should be eliminated from schools to help tackle the nation's obesity epidemic.

American Academy of Pediatrics

Hallelujah Kids

"In Virginia, for example, 276 juvenile delinquents at a detention facility housing particularly hardened adolescents were put on a diet that contained no sugar or chemical additives for two years. During that time, the incidence of theft dropped 77 percent, insubordination dropped 55 percent, and hyperactivity dropped 65 percent."
John Robbins at *Healthy Lifestyle Conference 2003*

For adolescents, especially African American adolescents, caffeine intake may increase blood pressure and thereby increase the risk of hypertension. Alternatively, caffeinated drink consumption may be a marker for dietary and lifestyle practices that together influence blood pressure..
Archive Pediatric Adolescent Med. 2004

The Causes of Health

It seems that society is so concerned about the causes and treatments of diseases that they overlook the causes of health which when applied reduce the need for treatments! So, what are these causes of health?

Trusting in God
Plant-Based Nutrition
Fresh, Pure Water
Fresh, Clean Air
Daily Vigorous Exercise
Regular Sunlight Exposure
Adequate Rest and Sleep
Loving Relationships

Trusting in God

Trust in the Lord with all thine heart; and lean not on thine own understanding. In all thy ways acknowledge him, and he shall direct thy paths. Be not wise in thine own eyes; fear the Lord, and depart from evil. It shall be health to thy navel, and marrow to thy bones.

Proverbs 3:5-8

Plant-Based Nutrition

Plant-based nutrition is what we believe God had in mind when he placed Adam & Eve in the Garden of Eden. Personally, I think He allowed the eating of animals after the flood as a means for survival. Fortunately, we are not living in survival mode anymore. Today we have fruits and vegetables available to us from all over the world! Besides, Daniel proved thousands of years ago that eating vegetables makes us look healthier and perform better than those who eat "royal food"-meat!

> "When barely 100 nutrients were known to man, it was estimated that there might be as many as 300. Now that thousands are known, it is estimated that there are at least as many as 100,000."
> Dr. Doug Graham www.doctorgraham.cc

> *And out of the ground made the Lord God to grow every tree that is*
> *pleasant to the sight, and good for food.*
>
> *Genesis 2:9*

Fresh, Pure Water

Our bodies are 75% water with our brains being 85% water! We lose approximately 10 glasses worth of water daily through the kidneys, colon, skin and breathing. The best way to replace this water is through drinking plenty of fresh, pure water and eating raw plant foods especially juicy fruits and vegetable juices.

> Mercury is one of the most dangerous toxins released from coal-fired power plants. When mercury pollution falls to the Earth in the form of rain and snow, it contaminates our lakes and rivers. Once in the water, the most toxic form of mercury - methylmercury - is absorbed by fish. Mercury contamination has become so widespread in this country, that 44 states warn residents to limit their consumption of fish - especially children and pregnant women.
> Greenpeace Action Network www.greenpeace.org

Pollution from industry, agriculture, prescription, over-the-counter drugs and more has invaded our water supply. It is estimated that soon, we will be recycling 100% of our nation's water having limited sources of fresh water available already. Our water treatment plants are simply not equipped to handle this workload.

Distilled and reverse osmosis purified water are clear choices for drinking water. Water treated with UV and Oxygen then filtered is another viable option.

> *For the Lamb which is in the midst of the throne shall feed them,*
> *and shall lead them unto living fountains of waters: and God shall*
> *wipe away all tears from their eyes.*
>
> *Revelation 7:17*

> Rain water has been naturally distilled by the heat of the sun but it becomes contaminated as it falls through air filled with bacteria, dust, smoke, chemicals, and minerals. By the time it reaches the earth as rain water, it is so saturated with decaying matter, dirt and chemicals that its color becomes a yellowish-white. Snow is even dirtier.
> *God's Way to Ultimate Health* by Dr. George Malkmus

Fresh, Clean Air

The most important element on earth is oxygen. Without it, human life simply could not exist. Humans can live for weeks without water, and go without food for months, but without oxygen, life could only carry on for a little while.

The respiratory system is the system of the body that deals with breathing. When we breathe, the body takes in the oxygen that it needs and removes the carbon dioxide that it doesn't need.

Every minute of every day you breathe in air. Without it you could live only a few minutes. The air that you breathe is oxygen. Oxygen is the most important part of the air. All animals and plants need it, too.

And the Lord God formed man of the dust of the ground,
and breathed into his nostrils the breath of life; and man became
a living soul.

Genesis 2-7

Daily Vigorous Exercise

Our kids need to get outside and PLAY! And since we are doing The Hallelujah Diet® along with them, we need to play alongside them!

The best way to increase oxygen in the body is through vigorous playful activities. Kids should be given much time to play-inside, outside, and upside down! We're not talking video games and computer games, we're talking good old-fashioned getting' dirty & sweaty games-you remember the kind that leave grass stains on your knees!

Moms share your rebounder (mini-trampoline) with the kids-no more monkeys jumpin' on the bed!

A merry heart doeth good like a medicine: but a broken
spirit drieth the bones.

Proverbs 17:22

Hallelujah Kids

Hallelujah Kids Can Exercise. . .

I started the Hallelujah Diet when I was 12 and I don't think I've ever made a better decision! Some friends were doing the Hallelujah Diet and told my mom and me about it. We decided it was time for a change! I didn't like the carrot juice or BarleyMax at first but now I crave it every day! I feel the best I EVER have and would NEVER go back to the way I was eating before! My body is even starting to crave more raw than cooked foods. My complexion has cleared up, I don't get bad headaches anymore, and my weight is better proportioned. I'm so blessed to be able to eat this way!

I have a praise report! I have always had a hard time with exercise. Recently, I started with jumping 10 times a day with a jump rope and now...I jump rope every day-I do it on one foot and I'm working on switching feet...I do 10 or more sit ups a day...I just got a resistance tube and I do two different exercises at 10 times each everyday (OUCH!!!). Then, I stretch my legs and attempt a split! I have never been able to do one so my goal is to practice every day until I can! Then I want to get an exercise ball but that just shows you that starting off small is better than not starting at all! I hope this encourages someone. THANK YOU MOM AND JULIE for pushing me!

Heather Q., 14
North Carolina

In a recent report issued by the U.S. Surgeon General's office, young women are being warned they, too, are susceptible to early stages of osteoporosis. Osteopenia, the precursor to the bone-crippling disease typical in post-menopausal women, is called the "young women's epidemic."

Dr. Bryant, American Council on Exercise's chief exercise physiologist, says bone-loading exercises and eating a high-calcium, high-fiber, low-fat diet is essential to building stronger bones. "Bone-loading or exercises that twist, bend, stretch or compress bones, can strengthen common at-risk areas including the upper shoulder, spine and forearm at the wrist. Lack of exercise is an all-too-common risk that can be easily prevented in young women." Preventative measures should start during the early teen years. Contrary to popular belief, osteoporosis is not an old woman's disease. In reality, it is a disease process that begins relatively early in life but does not manifest itself until later in life.

The American Council on Exercise www.acefitness.org

Regular Sunlight Exposure:

Benefits of:
Hormone Balancing
Vitamin Production
Blood Purification
Proper Sleep Cycling
Health for the Eyes

Every year, by May, my boys and I are tan. People always ask where we went for vacation. "Outside" is our answer! We don't burn because we respect the sun and tan on purpose. Sunshine is the best source for vitamin D, a pro-hormone that is essential for strong bones and a healthy body.

We don't use sunscreen; we use our brains, clothing and carrot juice which stimulates production of melanin in the skin helping to protect us from harmful rays. When we plan to be outside for long periods of time in the heat of the day, we protect ourselves with hats and cool, loose, thin, cotton clothing and the shade of a tree!

Sunscreen has not been shown to reduce the risk of melanoma [Dennis et al., 2003]. According to Dr. Holick's book, "The UV Advantage," SPF 8 reduces Vitamin D production by 97.5 percent and SPF 15 reduces it by 99.9 percent. This blocks out the sun that humans need to produce Vitamin D. It is estimated that up to 95% of Americans are vitamin D deficient at some point during the year.

Symptoms of vitamin D deficiency in children include weak bones, bone pain, muscle weakness and depression.

> The cancer risk has been debunked - sunlight does not trigger deadly basil-cell melanoma; genetic risk factors and irresponsible tanning leading to a sunburn does.
>
> *Cancer Journal - Journal of the National Cancer Institute,* Vol. 95, No. 20, October15, 2003, pp 1530-1538

For the Lord God is a sun and shield: the Lord will give grace and glory: no good thing will be withheld from them that walk upright.

Psalm 84:11

Adequate Rest and Sleep

> Children require 9 hours and 15 minutes of sleep each night while teens need 10 hours of sleep each night. Sleep deprivation can impair memory and inhibit creativity making it difficult for sleep-deprived students to learn. Teens struggle to learn to deal with stress and control emotion — sleep deprivation makes it even more difficult. Irritability, lack of self-confidence and mood swings are often common in a teen, but sleep deprivation makes it worse. Depression can result from chronic sleep deprivation. Not enough sleep can endanger their immune system and make them more susceptible to serious illnesses.
>
> Stanford University Online Health Library

Come unto me all ye that labour and are heavy laden, and I will give you rest.

Matthew 11-28

Loving Relationships

Hereby perceive we the love of God, because he laid down his life for us: and we ought to lay down our lives for our brethren.
1 John 3:16

And this is his commandment; that we should believe on the name of his Son Jesus Christ, and love one another, as he gave us commandment.
1 John 3:23

Blessed be God, even the Father of the Lord Jesus Christ, the Father of mercies, and the God of all comfort; who comforteth us in all our tribulation, that we may be able to comfort them which are in any trouble, by the comfort wherewith we ourselves are comforted of God.
2 Corinthians 1:3-4

Children, indeed, all of us need loving relationships. We need relationships with people of all ages and ethnicities in which we freely give and receive love. Volunteering to serve is a wonderful way children can live out this love for others.

The Hallelujah Diet® *for Kids*

One of the most frequently asked questions regarding The Hallelujah Diet®, especially The Hallelujah Diet® for kids, is WHAT DO YOU EAT? Answer: a lot!

For example:

Pre-Breakfast: 2-8 ounces (depending on age of child) carrot/apple/ veggie Juice—2/3 carrot, 1/3 greens, pieces of apple and BarleyMax®.

Breakfast: fresh fruits, homemade granolas, or whole grains

Mid-Morning: trail mixes with raw nuts, seeds, organic unsulphured dried fruits, more carrot/veggie juice, smoothies, veggie sticks with raw nut/seed butters, or fresh fruits

Lunch: raw nut butter sandwiches, fresh fruits, salads, soups, beans, or raw veggies on pitas/sprouted whole grain bread, hummus

Mid-Afternoon: trail mixes with raw nuts, seeds, organic unsulphured dried fruits, more carrot/veggie juice, smoothies, veggie sticks with raw nut/seed butters, or fresh fruits

Supper: salads, steamed vegetables (heavy emphasis on greens) soups, baked potatoes, squashes, or bean dishes

Evening: raw snacks, smoothies, fresh fruits or more juice

The Hallelujah Diet® *for Kids* Explained

For optimal nutrition, we would like to see kids eating approximately 50 percent of their foods in the raw, uncooked form with the remaining 50 percent being steamed vegetables, cooked whole grains, beans, soups and stews.

Beverages: freshly extracted vegetable juices, barley grass powder, distilled water, smoothies

Dairy Alternatives: fresh raw almond milk, creamy banana milk, sugar-free rice milk, non-dairy cheese without casein

Fruit: all fresh, as well as unsulphured organic dried fruit, fresh fruit juice and unsweetened frozen fruit

Grains: unrefined whole grains and sprouted grains

Nuts and Seeds: raw almonds, sunflower seeds, ground flax seeds, macadamia nuts, walnuts, pecans, pumpkin seeds, sesame seeds, hemp seeds, hazelnuts, cashews, raw nut butters and tahini

Oils and Fats: extra virgin olive oil, flax seed oil, avocadoes, mayonnaise made from cold-pressed oils

Seasonings: fresh or dried herbs, garlic, sweet onions, parsley, salt-free seasonings, light gray Celtic unrefined sea salt, salt-free vegetable broth

Vegetables: all raw vegetables, steamed, frozen, baked root vegetables and squashes

Sweeteners: raw unfiltered honey (honey should not be used for children under 12 months of age), rice syrup, unsulphured molasses, stevia, carob, pure maple syrup, dates and date sugar

While this list at first appears limited, there are hundreds if not thousands of exciting recipes that meet these criteria. See the recipe section of this book.

Why 50% Raw and Uncooked?

"Life on earth starts to die at 107 degrees! If a person has a fever of 106 degrees we get very concerned. At 107 degrees, brain cells start to break down and die, and when the internal temperature reaches 108 degrees the person dies. Well, plant life starts to die at 107 degrees also (the enzymes, life force, etc.), and by 122 degrees, the enzymes are dead and the life force is gone. For proof, take a raw carrot, cut off its top, place it in a shallow saucer of water, and watch it grow. Then take a carrot and boil, steam or bake it, then cut off the top of that cooked carrot. Place the cooked carrot top in a shallow saucer of water and it will no longer grow. Man is the only member of the animal kingdom created by God that cooks his/her food before eating it."

Rev. George Malkmus www.hacres.com

Why 50% Cooked?

Cooking certain foods makes them easier for kids to eat in abundance ensuring they get adequate calories and overall nutrition. Beans, for example, are nutrient-rich but not very appetizing raw! Kids have a better time eating dark green leafy vegetables when they are steamed or in soups making them easier to chew.

Specific "Food" to be Avoided

The following "foods" create most of the physical problems we experience and are not a part of The Hallelujah Diet®. They should be eliminated from the diet as quickly as possible.

Beverages: alcohol, coffee, tea, cocoa, carbonated beverages and soft drinks, all artificial fruit drinks, including sports drinks, and all commercial juices containing preservatives, salt and sweeteners

Dairy: all milk, cheese, eggs, ice cream, whipped toppings, and non-dairy creamers with the possible exception of raw goat milk products for infants unable to nurse

Fruit: canned and sweetened fruits, along with non-organic dried fruits

Grains: refined, bleached flour products, cold breakfast cereals, and white rice

Meats: beef, pork, fish, chicken, turkey, hamburgers, hot dogs, bacon, sausage, etc.

All meats are harmful to the body and the cause of up to 90 percent of all physical problems.
Rev. George Malkmus

Nuts & Seeds: all roasted and/or salted seeds and nuts (Peanuts are not a nut but a legume and very difficult to digest.)

Oils: all lard, margarine and shortenings and anything containing hydrogenated or partially hydrogenated oils

Seasonings: table salt, black pepper and any seasonings containing them

Soups: all canned, packaged or creamed soups containing dairy products

Sweets: all refined white or brown sugar, sugar syrups, chocolate, candy, gum, cookies, donuts, cakes, pies, or refined sugars or artificial sweeteners

Vegetables: all canned vegetables, or vegetables fried in oil

Hallelujah Kids

So, Where *Do* We Get Our Protein on The Hallelujah Diet®?

So glad you asked! The Hallelujah Diet® is not just your average vegetarian diet! We not only remove animal foods, we include lots of health- promoting foods! We don't just live on potatoes and spaghetti, although they are kid favorites (always make the salad come first!). The idea is to give them a variety of plant foods year round.

> When your calorie needs are met, your protein needs are met.
> Dr. Joel Fuhrman, *Eat to Live*, p 139

Keep in mind that our kids need more calories than we do. If they are very active or athletic, they will need even more! When serving plant foods, remember that, per volume, they are much lower in calories than animal sourced foods so the kids will be eating a good amount of food and maybe even more often than before. Don't be surprised when they come back two hours after eating asking for a snack. Toss them a couple apples with a handful of nuts and send them on their way! Encourage them to eat when they are hungry and do something else when they are not.

Dr. Joel Fuhrman states that it is unnecessary to combine foods to achieve protein completeness at each meal.

> The body stores and releases the amino acids needed over a 24-hour period. About 1/6 of our daily protein utilization comes from recycling our own body tissue. This recycling, or digesting our own cells lining the digestive tract, evens out any variation from meal to meal in amino acid "incompleteness." It requires no level of nutritional sophistication to get sufficient protein, even if you eat only plant foods.
> Dr. Joel Fuhrman, *Eat to Live*, p 137

In *The China Study*, we find the question, "What protein consistently and strongly promoted cancer? Casein, which makes up 87 percent of cow's milk protein, promoted all stages of the cancer process. The safe proteins were from plants..." (Campbell, p 6)

Moms, keep your eyes open for this dangerous milk protein called casein, when shopping for alternatives to dairy products. Unfortunately, you will find this substance in many alternative cheeses.

List of protein-rich plant foods included in The Hallelujah Diet®:

Spinach
Broccoli
Brussels sprouts
Kale
Lentils
Peas & Beans
Cabbage
Carrots
Corn
Potatoes
Tomatoes
Almonds
Almond Butter
Flax Seeds
Tahini
Sunflower Seeds
Pumpkin Seeds
Sprouted Whole Grain Breads
Cooked or Sprouted Brown Rice
Bananas
Barley Grass Powder

Believe it or not, kids can eat AND like these real foods! Check out the recipes in the recipe section for some great ideas on how to incorporate them into your daily menu.

Crack baby now a healthy 5-year-old Hallelujah Kid

We adopted two boys through the foster care system. Our younger son Christopher (Topher) was a crack baby. Not only did Topher test positive at birth for crack but he also had LSD, PCP and nine other amphetamines that I can't spell or pronounce in his system. At three weeks old we were told he most likely would never walk or talk. We were told also at three weeks that if he lived to the age of two, he would be on dialysis or have to have a kidney transplant. His kidney function was less than 30 percent and the doctors said that it was inevitable that he would have kidney failure. Topher also had epilepsy and was on medication for that. In addition to a very weak immune system, Topher had pneumonia nearly a dozen times in the first three years of life.

He was three when we began the Hallelujah Diet. At 5 years old and after implementing our lifestyle change, Topher does not require any breathing treatments! His kidney function is over 90 percent! He shows no signs of seizures! Not one bout of pneumonia! His eyesight has improved each time he has been back to the optometrist!

He tells me almost daily that he only wants me to give him healthy food. His favorites are salad with baby spinach leaves, roma tomatoes and Italian dressing. He also loves raw broccoli and cauliflower florets with a little honey, Veganaise™, and sunflower seeds.

Kim E. about Topher, 5

Topher

Broccoli has been around for more than 2000 years. The name "broccoli" comes from the Latin word brachium, which means "branch" or "arm." Americans have grown it in their gardens for only about 200 years! The first commercially grown broccoli was grown and harvested in New York, then planted in the 1920's in California. A few crates were sent back East and by 1925 the broccoli market was off the ground. This vegetable is highly recognized for its anti-cancer nutrients. It is a cruciferous vegetable and member of the cabbage family which is helpful in preventing certain types of cancer.

Food Traditions

Many of us follow food traditions. You know, cake and ice cream at birthday parties, going out to lunch for fried chicken after church on Sunday, taking the team out for ice cream after the ballgame. It's time to create some new traditions!

Since we buy most everything by the case, We always have an abundance of fresh food.

Each Sunday during the winter months, I bring oranges for my Sunday School class. One little guy told me he has "8-foot-big oranges" at his house. I asked him to bring me one some day-I'd like to see that! I always have at least 25 four year olds reaching out for orange sections like little baby birds! They can consume a huge box of seedless grapes in 10 minutes. Providing snacks like these might seem to cost a bit more than bringing 2 liter bottles of pop and biggie chips but, does it really?

We want to be careful not to encourage emotional connections to food. While we have fun food traditions, I try not to reward, bargain, threaten, comfort or soothe the kids with foods.

Hallelujah Kids

Toddlers on parade at a 2-year-old birthday party

Instead of cake and ice cream, Jerrod and Nikki served guests of their 2-year-old birthday girl blueberries and cream (frozen blueberries and rice milk, that is). The kids never missed the traditional sweets, parents report, especially since they were so busy decorating their wheeled vehicles—wagons, bikes, motorized cars—for the big birthday parade. Sounds like fun!

Jerrod S.

We like to frequent ethnic stores and restaurants. We get great produce at Oriental markets like cabbages, snow peas, baby bananas, mangos, Chinese broccoli, sprouts, hot peppers, durian and young coconuts. At Middle Eastern shops and restaurants we buy hummus, tabouli, baba ganoush, whole wheat pita bread, fresh olives and pine nuts. Wednesdays are vegetarian day at our favorite shop. Besides getting great food at better prices, we have built wonderful relationships with the owners of these small ventures.

For birthday dinners, we usually go to a favorite Middle Eastern restaurant for salads and hummus. Ryan loves fruit so he gets to pick out which ones to serve at his parties. We stick candles in watermelons for our cakes!

Shopping at farm markets makes for fun summer food traditions also. Riding through the apple orchard on a wagon to our favorite spot every fall rewards us with the very best apples!

Suggestions for Transitioning Kids

Making changes...

Making changes in diet after a lifetime of following the standard American diet can be challenging. A transitional diet is one where you make the changes in diet in stages. Here are some suggested baby steps for transitioning your kids to the Hallelujah Diet:

Include more fruits and vegetables to their diets each day. Begin each meal with some fruit or a salad and then eat the old stuff for a while.

Eliminate soda pop as soon as possible. Try water with lemon or have a little fruit juice (at least initially). Purchase a good juicer and juice a couple times a week and then work up to more.

Switch to whole-grain breads (100 percent stone-ground whole wheat) or sprouted bread. Consider baking your own bread from freshly milled flour.

Make changes one meal at a time. For breakfast, try some fresh fruit, followed by homemade granola. Have a big vegetable salad with some seeds or nuts for lunch. Sample some vegetarian cooked meals to serve after the salad for supper.

Offer raw food first, then the cooked. The transition may include some resistance and negative comments. If you make the changes along with your kids, it will be easier for them to follow your example. You can do this radically as some have, or make changes over time.

Annmarie, mom of five
Hallelujah Kids

Equip your army's soldiers to beat the bad guys as explained to son John

White blood cells are our army to defend us against the bad guys like germs, bacteria, and viruses. When we eat sugar, it makes the soldiers in our army go to sleep, so there's no one there to protect us from the bad guys. (Sugar has actually been snuck into enemy camps to weaken the armies!) When we eat good foods like fruits, vegetables, fresh juices, it's like giving our soldiers ammunition. The good things in good foods stop the bad guys. Drinking water helps the soldiers move faster and get around more easily.

Kim W., Health Minister[sm]

A word about power struggles…

If you want your children to drink a juice in the morning or eat some salad at dinner, make it clear that they will need to finish that item before any other food is going to be had. "When you're done with your juice,…" "When you've had your salad,…"

When you treat this as matter of fact and don't become emotionally involved in a power struggle, your children will quickly learn it's up to them how quickly they get on to a preferred food. In time it will become a habit. Some of us are blessed with strong-willed children who decide it's all-out war and refuse to eat the new healthful foods. Do not enter into a power struggle with them. Do not threaten, argue, or bribe. Just make it clear that these are the foods that are offered, and none others will be available until these have been had. And leave it up to them. Be careful you don't get drawn into the struggle. They may miss one meal. They may even miss two. They might even go to bed hungry. But how many times do you think this will happen? Better some short-term discomfort for the long-term benefits of their understanding your expectations.

Kim W., Health Minister[sm]

When it comes to carrot juice, packaging is everything . . .

As delicious as carrot juice is, it might take some getting used to. Try these suggestions for bringing kids on board:

1. Begin with freshly made apple juice and gradually add more and more carrot juice.
2. Use a special cup that is just for their "special juice." A colored cup may be helpful in disguising the color of the juice.
3. Try marketing the juice not as carrot juice (eewww!) but as "power juice" made especially for them. Other ideas are "Johnny Juice," "Superboy Juice," "Princess Beauty Juice." You get the idea.

This scripture might be helpful on your refrigerator, to encourage you to stick to your guns. You are training your child to eat foods that will protect their health. This scripture may encourage you to wait for their hunger. A common scenario that plays out in many households is (I bet you've said it yourself):

"Mom, I'm hungry."

"There are apples, raisins and nuts in the fridge."

"No, I don't want that."

"Then you must not be that hungry."

A truly hungry child (and adult) will be content with healthful foods.

Kim W., Health Minister[sm]

Hallelujah Kids

What? No stove?

When I started a vegetarian diet I just announced one night that I would no longer be cooking meat. My husband continued to barbecue for a number of months but then he stopped.

When we remodeled our kitchen, we didn't replace the stove. Our kids were teenagers at the time and they've learned to live without cooking fire. After four years, we still don't have a stove.

Joe and I have been married for nearly 25 years. We have maintained a vegetarian diet for 15 years, seven of which have been on the Hallelujah Diet®. Our children are now 20 & 22 and very healthy. They eat a vegetarian, but not strictly raw diet. The best news of all is no one is on any medication.

Shari V., Health Minister[sm]

Taking The Hallelujah Diet® on the road

Every summer, the boys and I pack up and go camping for a week at a Christian music festival. We have discovered some great ways to stay on the diet during this event. We camp in a tent so we don't have refrigeration. I freeze carrot juice in big glass jars then use it for ice blocks. We drink off the juice as it thaws. It lasts a good three days. We then use carrot juice powder for the rest of the week. We bring our barley grass powder to mix with water and barley grass capsules for Corbin who won't drink the powder. We are able to buy ice at the festival so we keep everything on ice as much as possible.

Watermelon and cantaloupe travel well out of the cooler as long as you don't leave leftovers! I just cut them in half and provide forks with the watermelon and spoons with the cantaloupe. I bring big Ziploc bags full of lettuces for salads (just make sure it is nice and dry before packing it). I also bring other veggies to cut over the salads then store them in Ziplocs in the coolers. Berries and grapes also travel well if put in plastic ware then in the cooler.

Raw almond butter and sugarless jelly with sprouted grain bread is great for the kids' lunches. We sometimes make sprouted grain cinnamon raisin toast over the fire then put honey on it for breakfast. The boys like to have grilled veggies and baked potatoes some nights with our salads. We brought fresh corn on the cob this year, wet it down and put it on the grill. I think most all travel can be done on the diet with a bit of planning. We never leave home without food and water!

I even packed a duffle bag full of melons when I traveled out of state one year and asked the hotel chef to cut it for me as I needed it since I couldn't fly with a knife! (Meeting the chef got us great salads every night, too.)

Vegan junk food

As you incorporate more fruits and vegetables into their diets, some kids might respond better if they still get familiar looking foods like burgers, dogs and fries to go with that big bowl of coleslaw. If that's the case, check out the pre-packaged store-bought vegan "junk food" available now. It's much better now than it was thirty years ago! While these foods are not an actual part of The Hallelujah Diet®, they are great for transition and special situations!

Hallelujah Kids

Once in awhile for functions that the boys attend away from home, I let them bring snacks like organic chips instead of our traditional grapes and homemade trail mixes. When they have some of this food, they say they don't feel like they stand out quite so much.

Remember that with The Hallelujah Diet® we are not only looking for foods that are not harmful, we are primarily looking for foods that are extremely beneficial. So, while it is not as harmful to give the kids organic low fat baked potato chips rather than conventional ones, it is more beneficial to give them flax crackers.

> "Heart disease begins in the first five to ten years of life, when children get too much fat in their blood. The hidden danger for children is in potato chips, processed sweets, and candy, which are all full of greasy oil."
> Dr. Jay Gordon www.drjaygordon.com

Mankind was created from the dust of the earth. God intended for him to be nourished by the plants that grow from that very same dust, not "foods" that were formulated in man's laboratories.

Vegan junk food, processed pre-packaged store-bought food, is okay once in awhile, but it can be a dangerous trap for kids. We want them to desire foods in their God-given packaging, not pretty, colorful bags and boxes.

> To burn off one plain M&M™ candy, you need to walk the full length of a football field.
> www.acefitness.org

Pain relief…

I have been on the Hallelujah Diet for two and a half months. It is not so bad. I have found different kinds of vegetables that I like. I really like to eat our new creation sandwich of whole grain bread or Ezekiel bread with nut butter, honey, banana and sunflower seeds. My mom and brother add raisins.

I gave up powder mix drinks, sugar, flour, all dairy and fried foods. I only have meat once every other day. I have lost 23 pounds. I feel better and have more energy. I have been taking TaeKwonDo with my entire family for the last two and a half months and am an orange belt now. My face has been clearing up and I do not have migraines anymore. My JRA (juvenile rheumatoid arthritis) does not hurt as much.

I like to eat fruit and the carrot juice is okay. I like carrot juice with sweet potato in it. Some of my favorite things to eat now are sweet potatoes, meatless chili, meatless spaghetti, and bean burritos. Salads are okay, too.

I wanted to do The Hallelujah Diet with my parents because of my JRA. I don't want to be crippled one day.

> Jesse B., 13
> North Carolina

Recipes

Kid Tested - Mother & Hallelujah Acres® Approved!

Juice for Hallelujah Kids (and their parents)

Kids love juice! Following are recipes that satisfy thirst and so much more. Purchase all organic produce for your juice whenever possible. Before proceeding with any of the juice recipes, thoroughly wash and rinse all produce. Please feel free to sneak in some celery or romaine lettuce!

Carrot Juice

Carrots

Juiced in a juicer! You can add slices of apple if the kids want it sweeter. Remove carrot greens before juicing.

Carrot juice is the cornerstone of The Hallelujah Diet®. Daily we drink juice made from carrots oftentimes adding green vegetables and apples. Carrot juice is very nutrient-rich with calcium, beta carotene, vitamin C, potassium, magnesium, manganese, thiamin, iron, copper, zinc, and more!

> *Two carrots are riding in a car and they get into a terrible accident. They're rushed to a hospital. One carrot has only scrapes and bruises, but the other carrot is rushed to surgery. Hours later the doctor comes out and says to the first carrot, I have good news and bad news. The good news is that your friend is going to live. The bad news is that he's going to be a vegetable for the rest of his life.*

Apple Romaine Barley Grass Juice

from Ryan W., 10

24 apples
2 large heads romaine lettuce

Juice the apples and romaine lettuce. Pour into 12-ounce glass jars with lids (mason jars work well) and store in the fridge. When you're ready to drink it, add 1 tsp. barley grass powder, shake and enjoy.

---

2 year old loves barley grass powder...

I've raised both my kids, ages 2 years and 10 months, on the Hallelujah Diet from the very beginning. They have never had sugar and live for barley grass powder and carrot juice. My 2 year old asks for barley grass powder raw out of the container. She loves it. When she plays, pretending to serve refreshments, it is always carrot juice or barley grass that she makes. My 10 month old has never been sick. I'm so blessed to have the knowledge of this wonderful diet and lifestyle. I try to share it with as many people as I can.

Mommy of Alexis and Ashton

Grape Juice

Juice bunches of grapes—all one kind or a variety. Juice a few stalks of celery in there and the kids will never know. Shhh.

> The grape is one of the oldest fruits to be cultivated going back as far as Biblical times. Spanish explorers introduced the fruit to America approximately 300 years ago.
>
> Concord grapes are one of only three fruits native to North America. The other two: blueberries and cranberries.
>
> "Fun with Fruit Facts," *Fruit Grower*, December 1997

Pineapple Juice

1 ripe pineapple

Peel and core the pineapple and juice in the juicer. Now, that's fresh pineapple juice!

Pineapple Strawberry Juice

1 ripe pineapple
20 strawberries

Peel and core the pineapple. Remove tops of strawberries.
Juice in the juicer. So pretty.

Pineapple Red Pepper Juice

1 ripe pineapple
1 red bell pepper

Peel and core the pineapple then juice it with the stemmed and seeded red bell pepper.

Hallelujah Kids

Pineapples originally grew in South America. The pineapple plant was spread over tropical areas by the Spanish and Portuguese, and it was also taken back to Europe to be grown there. Europeans developed pineapple plantations, improved the plant, and brought it to Hawaii and Australia. Today, China produces the most pineapples in the world.

Pineapples can be grown by placing the top green of the fruit into soil.

Orange Carrot Juice

5 carrots

2 oranges

Juice the carrots in the juicer and the oranges by hand or with an electric citrus juicer. Mix together.

Hallelujah kid prefers carrot juice…

Our daughter Ariel is almost 3 years old. I first heard about the Hallelujah diet when she was 8 months old, however prior to that, she was only breast fed and I had just started introducing organic food to her. I began giving her barley grass powder in a couple ounces of water at 8 months old. She now prefers Barley Max dry! (I can't even take it dry.) We also began juicing carrots and she prefers it to any other drink now.

When Ariel was about 25 months, she caught the chicken pox. Ariel's chicken pox experience was absolutely amazing. During the 6 days that she had the spots, she never scratched them at all. She had all her energy, and wasn't down at all. The only symptom Ariel had was the spots. I continued giving Ariel carrot juice, barley grass powder and raw foods the entire time.

Ariel is very tall for the age of 3, and many people have asked if she is 4 or 5 years old. She is bright, alert, has an incredible memory and is full of spunk and energy. We are extremely pleased with the health of our daughter and the choices we have made for her as a result of incorporating the Hallelujah Diet and making it a lifestyle for our family.

from John and Candy G.
Dundas, Ontario, Canada

Salsa Juice

4-6 juicy ripe tomatoes
1 lime
3 sprigs fresh cilantro
1 sliver garlic
1/2 a red bell pepper
1 sliver of jalapeno or dash of hot sauce

Juice all ingredients except the lime in the juicer. Squeeze the lime in by hand.

Hallelujah Kids

Mom's Weight Loss Juice

1 large kohlrabi with leaves, unpeeled
1-3 pounds of carrots
4 stalks celery
1 apple

A great meal replacement for us moms watching our weight! Store leftovers in a glass jar in the fridge and drink it later in the day.

Everyday Juice

5 pounds carrots
1 small beet with greens
1 stalk celery
2 green leaves—kale, collards, spinach or turnip
2 apples

Juice all in the juicer. Store in 8 or 12-ounce serving containers (mason jars work well) filled to the top and sealed. Most nutritious if used within 24 hours.

Christmas Juice

3 pounds apple
1 pound cranberries
3 pounds oranges
Dash cinnamon (optional)

Juice the apples and cranberries in the juicer and the oranges with a citrus juicer or by hand. Mix together and serve. For a lovely Christmas morning serving arrangement, pour juice into a punch bowl and float orange slices, cranberries and ice cubes.

Lemon/Lime Juice

1 apple
1/2 inch fresh ginger (less if you find the taste too strong)
Handful of grapes
1/4 lemon
1/2 lime

Juice the apple, ginger and grapes in the juicer. Juice the lemon and lime by hand then mix together.

Next time you have a sore throat, reach for a lemon! Add the juice of one lemon to an equal amount of hot water for an anti-bacterial gargle.
Sunkist www.sunkist.com

Fruit Punch

1 apple
6 strawberries
Half an orange

Juice the apple and strawberries in the juicer. Juice the orange by hand then mix together. This is sooooo good!

Pineapple/Strawberry/Grape Juice

1 pineapple, peeled
2 pints strawberries, hulled
1 bunch green or red grapes
2 stalks celery

Juice all ingredients in the juicer.

Hallelujah Kids

Apple Berry Juice

4-6 apples
A couple handfuls of berries, any kind

Juice all together.

> It is a good idea to eat apples with their skin. Almost half of the vitamin C content is just underneath the skin. Eating the skin also increases insoluble fiber content. Most of an apple's fragrance cells are also concentrated in the skin and as they ripen, the skin cells develop more aroma and flavor.
> University of Illinois Extension

8 Vegetable Juice

1/2 tomato
1/4 cucumber
1 carrot
1 celery stalk
1 handful of spinach
1/2 red pepper
1/2 cup cabbage
1 green onion

Juice all ingredients in the juicer. To spice it up, add a few drops of hot sauce or cayenne pepper and juice in a tiny sliver of garlic.

Popeye Juice

5 bundles of spinach
1 cucumber
2 carrots

Juice all ingredients in the juicer.

Apple Kiwi Juice

> 2 apples
> 2 kiwi fruit, unpeeled
> 2 pears, unpeeled
> 1 stalk celery

Juice all ingredients in the juicer.

Apple Kiwi Spinach Juice
from Susan E.

> 2 apples
> 2 kiwi fruit, unpeeled
> 1 bunch of spinach

Juice all ingredients in the juicer.

Kiwi Mandarin Juice

> 5 kiwi fruit, unpeeled
> 5 mandarin oranges

Juice the kiwis in the juicer. Juice the mandarin oranges by hand or with a citrus juicer. Mix together and serve.

Legend has it that mandarin oranges were named for their resemblance, in shape and color, to the buttons atop the hats worn by those officials of the Chinese empire.
Friendly Press, Inc., 1984.

Hallelujah Kids

Grandma's Lemon Mango Juice
from Gloria E., R.N. and Health Minister[sm]

> 1 mango
> 2 lemons

Juice the mango in the juicer and the lemons by hand. Mix together and serve.

Super Citrus

> 1 Valencia orange
> 1 mandarin orange
> 1 tangerine
> 1 grapefruit
> 1 lemon

Using an electric citrus juicer or by hand, juice all ingredients.

Christopher Columbus brought the first orange seeds and seedlings to the New World on his second voyage in 1493.
Sunkist www.sunkist.com

Blood Orange Juice

> Blood oranges

Juice by hand or with a citrus juicer.

Moro oranges are also called blood oranges! But don't worry. That's just because the pulp is bright red. They're really a sweet treat.
Sunkist www.sunkist.com

Juicesicle

Using your favorite juice recipe, put in molds with popsicle sticks and freeze. Breakfast or anytime.

Green Juice

> 1 bunch spinach
> 1/2 bunch parsley
> 5 stalks celery
> 2 apples
> Juice of 1 lemon

Run everything through the juicer except lemon & strain. Squeeze in lemon juice.

Lemonade

> 6 apples
> 1 bunch green grapes
> Juice of 2 lemons

Juice apples and grapes in a juicer then squeeze in lemon juice. Pour over ice.

Breakfast Recipes

Rice/Millet Blender Muffins

Each recipe makes one blender full, sufficient batter for a dozen muffins. Bake at 350 degrees for 25-30 minutes. It's best to mix one batch at a time. Blending the rice results in an aerated batter and a spongy consistency without being dry.

> 1-1/2 cups long grain brown rice
> 1/2 cup millet
> 1-1/2 cups water

Soak overnight. (Begins the germination process, breakdown of phytic acid, and makes the grains easier to blend. Also makes for fluffier muffins.)
To this grain and water add:

> 1 apple, cored and cut into chunks.
> 1 tsp Celtic Sea Salt
> 2-4 Tbsp extra virgin olive oil
> 1-3 Tbsp honey

Blend thoroughly until grain is only slightly gritty.

Add 1 Tbsp baking powder (aluminum-free) at the end and blend just until mixed.

Variations: Substitute corn for millet in equal proportions. Substitute one or two ripe bananas in place of apple. Add carob bean powder, or sweetened carob chips. Add chopped nuts.

Blender Pancakes

2 cups long grain brown rice
1 cup millet or corn
2-1/2 cups water

Soak overnight. (Begins the germination process, breakdown of phytic acid, and makes the grains easier to blend, especially the corn.)

To this grain and water add:

1 to 1-1/2 apples, cored and cut into chunks.
1 rounded tsp Celtic Sea Salt
2 Tbsp extra virgin olive oil
2 Tbsp honey

Blend thoroughly until grain is only slightly gritty.

Add 1-1/2 Tbsp baking powder (aluminum-free) baking powder at the end and blend just until mixed. Bake on a hot grill.

God cares about the little things, even waffles...

Some of my most meaningful memories as a little boy grow-ing up in Seattle, Washington, are of the hours that I spent with my mom in the kitchen creating all sorts of amazing meals, snacks, treats and baked items. One meaningful item that came from that time is a cook book that my mom bestowed upon me when I graduated from college. The other is a waffle iron. It is a dingy yellow waffle iron that makes plate-sized round waffles! The rear leg of three legs spins so it has to be adjusted with each use so it doesn't fall over when it stands open. The knob on the front that sets the cooking dark-ness hasn't been turned in many years but the red light that illuminates when the waffle is being cooked still works!

We didn't have waffles every week but those mornings we did were really special to me. I wanted to create special waffle memories with my son Gabe but I had a problem to deal with that created a fairly upsetting morning for me. I attempted to compile a recipe that would make as tasteful a waffle but not compromise The Hallelujah Diet, which I had followed for over four years.

I was diagnosed with stage 4 metastasized melanoma late in 1999 and told I had little chance of living many more years. I was also informed that I would never have children or race cars again. Thanks to our choice to fully adopt the Hallelujah Diet and Lifestyle, we have two beautiful children with one on the way and a successful racing career and we are empow-ered to teach and encourage others to reach for the same results in their health.

So creating a recipe that would align with the Hallelujah Lifestyle was important to me but equally important was the desire to create wonderful memories in my son's life like I have of my childhood. I actually found myself on my knees in prayer about, yes, waffles.

A couple weeks later, my wife, kids and, ironically enough, my mom loaded up for a road trip to visit with some friends, who are also associated with Hallelujah Acres. During our visit and without prompting, they suggested we give their pan-cakes a try. They were really good! They told us the recipe for waffles was similar and that they would share it with us! And, well, the rest is history! Thank you, Jesus, for caring about the little things.

Jerrod S., Health Minister &
Hallelujah Dad

Hallelujah Kids

Jerrod, Gabe, Farrell and Nikki

Blender Waffles

Note: This recipe can be used for pancakes. The thicker batter results in lighter, thicker pancakes. The ingredients in the amounts listed below will almost fill an 8-cup blender container.

> **3 cups long grain brown rice**
> **1 cup millet or corn**
> **3 cups water**

Soak overnight. (Begins the germination process, breakdown of phytic acid, and makes the grains easier to blend, especially the corn.)

To this grain and water add:

> **1-1/2 apples, cored and cut into chunks.**
> **1 rounded tsp Celtic Sea Salt**
> **4 Tbsp extra virgin olive oil**
> **2 Tbsp honey**

Blend thoroughly until grain is only slightly gritty.

Add 1-1/2 Tbsp baking powder (aluminum-free) at the end and blend just until mixed.

Raw Almond/Nut Milk

1/2 cup raw almonds or any other nuts

3 cups water to cover

2-5 soaked dates to taste (optional for making Sweet Almond Milk)

Soak nuts overnight in the refrigerator. Blend in blender with more water to desired consistency. Strain, using cheesecloth. Refrigerate. Use the same or next day.

Banana Milk

2-3 ripe bananas

1 quart water

1 stalk celery

Blend the bananas and celery in water until milky consistency. If this is for a baby bottle, add more water so it will come out of the bottle easily.

"Sports drinks are supposed to quench your thirst and supply necessary nutrients. Commercial formulas do neither job well. The simplest, healthiest and most effective sports drinks can be made very easily by blending a few bananas into a quart of water. This will supply the necessary water, sugar (glucose and fructose), and electrolytic minerals while providing adequate vitamins and enzymes to properly metabolize them. To supply extra electrolytes without adding extra sugar, add a stalk of celery to the blend."

Nutrition and Athletic Performance by Dr. Doug Graham

Hallelujah Kids

Cinnamon Cantaloupe
from Pam F.

1 cantaloupe, cut into bite size pieces
Sprinkle with cinnamon

Most people don't know that melons are in the same gourd family as squashes and cucumbers. Most melons have similar structure to winter squash with thick flesh and inner seed-filled midsection. So what's the difference between melons and squashes? It's the way that they're used. Squashes are considered vegetables, while melons are known as fruits with sweet and juicy flavor. Melons should be eaten alone - not mixed with other foods.

> Melons are a good source of vitamin C and potassium. They have high water content are relatively low in calories, and also fat and cholesterol free.
> www.5aday.com *The CDC's 5 A Day Program*

Fruit 'n' Cereal
from Nikki S.

As a breakfast:

Chop up a bunch of fruit into small pieces and mix it up in a large bowl. Distribute it into smaller bowls for serving. Pour a small amount of Kamut, millet and/or Kashi over the fruit. Chop up a raw living foods snack bar from Hallelujah Acres® (Mapel Nut Royale or Vanilla Nut Goodee) into small pieces and sprinkle over the top (optional). Pour a little almond milk over the mix.Sprinkle with coconut or drizzle with honey to taste.

As a treat/dessert:

Freeze fruit after chopping and mixing. Don't use cereal. Chill the serving bowl. Use even less almond milk (almond milk should be really cold and should stick to the fruit and freeze).

Five Fruit Salad

1 cup seedless grapes
1/2 cup each: orange, peeled, sliced and quartered
     cantaloupe, cubed
     banana, sliced
     pineapple, peeled, cored and cubed
1/4 cup orange juice concentrate
1 tsp lime juice
2 tsp mint leaves, chopped
1/4 tsp lime peel, grated

Mix all ingredients in a medium bowl and serve.

Mango Blueberry Nectarine Salad

1 large mango, peeled and diced
2 cups blueberries
2 nectarines, unpeeled and sliced

Mix in a bowl and serve.

Honey Orange Strawberry Salad

2 cups strawberries, hulled and halved
2 cups grapes
2 bananas, peeled and sliced
1 kiwi fruit, peeled and sliced
raw, unfiltered, unpastuerized honey

Mix in a bowl. Drizzle with raw honey and serve.

Honey Orange Sauce

> 1/3 cup fresh orange juice
> 2 Tbsp lemon juice
> 1-1/2 Tbsp honey
> 1/4 tsp ginger
> Dash nutmeg

Combine all ingredients for sauce and mix. Just before serving, pour Honey Orange Sauce over fresh fruit.

Granola

From Recipes for Life by Rhonda Malkmus

> 4 cups rolled oats
> 1 cup crushed almonds
> 1/2 cup whole grain flour
> 1 tsp cinnamon
> 1/4 cup shredded coconut
> 1 cup sunflower seeds
> 1/2 cup wheat germ
> 1 cup honey, sorghum, molasses or maple syrup
> 1 tsp vanilla
> 1 cup pumpkin seeds

To dehydrate your granola, rather than baking it: Grind pumpkin and sunflower seeds to a finer texture. In a large bowl combine with all of the other dry ingredients. In a separate bowl combine the wet ingredients. Combine and mix well. Place on solid dehydrator sheets and dehydrate until dry.

OR, Spread evenly on a non-stick cookie sheet. Bake 20 minutes in a preheated 250 degree oven, stir and continue to bake another 20 minutes, stirring periodically to prevent burning. The granola should be lightly browned. Remove from oven and serve warm or cool thoroughly and store in a tightly sealed container or plastic bags. Option: After granola has cooled, add organic raisins or other organic unsulphured dried fruits.

Serve with rice, banana or almond milk.

Chocolate Granola
from Ryan W., 10

4 cups old fashioned oats

1 cup chopped almonds

1 cup pumpkin seeds

1 cup sunflower seeds

1 cup chopped walnuts

1 cup chopped hazelnuts

1 cup unsulphured unsweetened shredded coconut

1/4 cup raw sugar (optional)

1/2 cup hempseeds

1/2 cup maple syrup

1/4 cup safflower or grape seed oil

1/4 cup organic cocoa powder or carob powder

Mix in a large bowl, lay granola out on cookie sheets and bake at 350 degrees for 15 minutes or dehydrate 4-6 hours. Cool and store in plastic bags in the refrigerator or freezer.

Apple Sauce
from Recipes for Life by Rhonda Malkmus

Almonds ground into small pieces

1/2 cup raw peeled apple cut into small pieces

1/2 ripe banana

This combination can be served as is or put through the Champion Juicer with the blank screen in to make a wonderful apple sauce. Serve with half a ripe banana cut into rounds. For variety, add a date while putting apples through the juicing machine.

Hallelujah Kids

Banana Bread
from Robin B. as seen in <u>*Healthy 4 Him, Recipes for HealThy Living*</u>

4-6 ripe bananas, mashed

2 Tbsp ground flax seeds soaked in water to cover

1 tsp vanilla

1/2 cup organic butter, melted

3 Tbsp rice milk mixed with 1 Tbsp raw apple cider vinegar

1-1/2 cup whole wheat pastry flour

1 cup turbinado or raw sugar

1 tsp baking soda

1/2 tsp Celtic Sea Salt

Mix bananas, flax, vanilla and butter. Stir in rice milk mix. Mix remaining ingredients together and add to banana mix. Grease pan with butter or use a non-stick pan and bake at 350 degrees for one hour.

Bananas from freezer to smoothie in a snap

Peel ripe bananas then seal them in a freezer bag. Place in freezer. The bananas will break apart easily and blend well when you are ready to add them to your favorite smoothie recipe.

Smoothies

Banana Almond Butter Smoothie (tastes better than a Reeses'Cup ™)
from Becky S.

2 cups carob Rice Dream™

3-4 frozen bananas

2 Tbsp raw almond butter

2 Tbsp maple syrup or honey

Make extra for popsicle treats later in week. The kids love them!

Mango Milkshake

> 4-6 mangos, flesh only
> 1 tsp cinnamon
> 6 ice cubes
> 1 cup raw almond milk
> 1/2 tsp vanilla

Blend all in blender.

All Raw Mango Milkshake

> Mangos-flesh only
> 1 tsp cinnamon
> 6 ice cubes
> 1 cup raw almond milk
> 1/2 vanilla bean flesh
> 1-2 dates

Blend all in blender.

Fruit Smoothies
from Trish M.

> Any variety of fruit
> A little beet juice for bright color
> Dried apricots or dates for sweetener

Put all ingredients in a blender and blend until mixed. Add ice cubes to thicken.

Hallelujah Kids

Pineapple, Banana and Blueberry Smoothie

1 cup pineapple, peeled, cored and cubed
1 frozen banana
1 cup rice or almond milk
1 cup blueberries, fresh or frozen

Place all ingredients in a blender and blend until mixed.

Orange Grape Smoothie

1 cup grapes
1 banana, peeled and sliced
1 orange, peeled and sectioned
6-8 ice cubes

Place all ingredients in a blender and blend until mixed.

Banana Strawberry Chocolate Smoothie
from Corbin W., 12

4 bananas, peeled and sliced
1-1/2 cups strawberries, hulled
1 stalk celery, chopped
2 ice cubes
1-2 cups almond or rice milk
Organic cocoa or carob powder to taste

Blend, adding milk as needed, and serve. If using frozen bananas, omit the ice cubes and increase the milk if necessary.

Banana Mango Smoothie

3-4 bananas
1 mango
1 stalk celery, chopped
4 ice cubes
1/2 - 1 cup water
1 Tbsp maple syrup or 2 pitted dates (optional)

Blend, adding water as needed, and serve. If using frozen bananas, omit the ice cubes and increase the water if necessary.

Peach Slushy

2 fresh ripe peaches, chopped
2 ice cubes
1 Tbsp maple syrup

Blend in a high power blender.

Strawberry Coconut Smoothie
from Renee F., Health Minister[SM]

1 young coconut meat and milk
5 pitted dates
3 frozen bananas
1 cup frozen strawberries
Half an avocado
1 tsp vanilla (optional)

Combine all ingredients and blend in the blender.

Hallelujah Kids

Banana Strawberry Smoothie

> 3 bananas
> 1-1/2 cup strawberries
> 1 stalk celery, chopped
> 2 ice cubes
> 1-2 cups vanilla almond or rice milk
> 1 Tbsp maple syrup or 2 pitted dates (optional)

Blend, adding milk as needed, and serve. If using frozen bananas, omit the ice cubes and increase the milk if necessary.

Grandma's Peach Smoothie
from Gloria E.

> 4 small or 2 large frozen bananas
> 6 peaches, unpeeled
> 4 dates, pitted
> 1/4 cup fresh pineapple juice or lemon juice
> Water to blend

Place all ingredients in blender and blend.

Cherry Banana Smoothie

> 3 bananas
> 1 cup cherries, pitted
> 1 stalk celery, chopped
> 2 ice cubes
> 1 cup vanilla almond or rice milk
> 1 Tbsp maple syrup or 2 pitted dates (optional)

Blend, adding milk as needed, and serve. If using frozen bananas, omit the ice cubes and increase the milk if necessary.

Blueberry Banana Smoothie

2 frozen bananas
2 fresh ripe bananas, peeled and sliced
1-1/2 cups frozen blueberries
1-2 cups vanilla rice milk
1 Tbsp maple syrup or 2 pitted dates (optional)

Blend, adding rice milk as needed, and serve.

Icy Banana Smoothie
from Ryan W., 9

4 frozen bananas
Water to cover, adding as needed to blend

Blend until icy.

Despite its creamy texture a banana contains only 1 gram of fat. In fact an average banana contains only 120 calories. And because it's so filling, is ideal for that mid-afternoon energy-boost.

Rena's Smoothies

I make smoothies quite often for my boys Spencer and Austin who are 4. There are three of us so I use 4 bananas, several handfuls of strawberries and a handful of raspberries. I usually use a rice milk base, throw in some freshly ground flax seeds and some bee pollen. I sometimes add carob for a chocolaty taste. Other times I use peaches or blueberries if I have them instead of the strawberries and raspberries. I find the blueberries really set up (gel) more than the other fruits so it gets really thick.

Spencer and Austin G.

Lunch

What to Pack for a Healthful Lunch

1. A vegetable, like carrots.
2. A grain product, like bread, tortilla chips, or cold pasta or rice salad
3. Nuts or seeds, like raw nuts OR nut butter on the bread (may include jam or honey), may add olives and legumes to this category)
4. A fruit, like an apple, peach, OR dried fruit, like apricots or raisins

Michaela B., 8, Ohio

Other favorite lunchbox treats are:

Tortilla chips or romain lettuce leaves with fresh salsa

Pita bread with hummus and cut veggies

Celery with raw nut butter

Cold pasta salad, rice salad, bean salad, potato salad, ANY kind of salad —
    add dressing right before eating.

Bowls of cut fruits or whole fruits

Baggies of trail mixes

Jars of carrot juice

Bottle of water

Dinner Recipes

One of the most frequently asked questions I get is, "What do you feed the kids for dinner?"

Sometimes we have breakfast for dinner. And why not? The selection is vast. When my boys come in from a full summer day of tennis in the hot sun, there is nothing better than a BIG frozen banana smoothie! Blending celery or romaine lettuce in smoothies is a great way to get it into the kids after a workout.

Many nights, dinner consists of a nice big salad followed by a great soup or stew. You will find several different salads and soups here that can be mixed and matched for awesome dinners! Add some whole wheat bread and dinner is served.

Salad

These are typical veggies we keep for salads:

Romaine lettuce
Leaf lettuces
Red bell peppers
Carrots
Onion
Radishes
Celery
Broccoli
Cauliflower
Cucumbers
Kohlrabi
Tomatoes

Hallelujah Kids

Italian Dressing

2/3 cup olive or flax oil (or combination)

3 Tbsp raw apple cider vinegar

2 Tbsp Italian Seasoning Herb Blend

1 tsp honey

1 clove garlic, pressed

Pinch Celtic Sea Salt (optional)

Mix all and shake in a jar. Let flavors blend for about an hour. Shake again and serve.

Basic Vinaigrette

1/4 cup olive oil

2 Tbsp lemon juice

1 tsp raw apple cider vinegar

2 tsp raw honey

1/2 tsp Dijon mustard

1 Tbsp fresh basil, chopped

1 Tbsp fresh thyme, chopped

Dash Celtic Sea Salt

Whisk all with a fork.

French Dressing

2/3 cup organic fruit-sweetened catsup

1/2 cup raw apple cider vinegar

3/4 cup raw honey

1/4 cup flax oil

1 small onion

2 tsp paprika

2 tsp vegetarian Worcestershire sauce (no sardines)

1/4 cup water or more to thin

Mix all in the blender or food processor until creamy. Makes a great veggie dip!

Honey Mustard Dressing

> 1 Tbsp Dijon mustard
> 1 Tbsp raw honey
> 1 Tbsp walnut, olive oil or flax oil
> 1 Tbsp hot water
> Dash hot sauce or pinch of cayenne (optional)

Whisk all with a fork. This is another great veggie dip. My boys like to pour this over stir-fried vegetables and rice too!

Sweet-n-Sour Dressing
from Corbin W., 12

> 1 small onion
> 1/2 tsp celery seed
> 1/2 tsp poppy seeds
> 3 Tbsp honey or maple syrup
> Juice of 1 lemon
> 1/4 cup olive oil

Put all in the food processor except the olive oil. Blend until creamy then drizzle in the olive oil.

When shopping for bottled salad dressings, look for ones with the fewest number of ingredients, low sodium, no hydrogenated or partially hydrogenated oils, few sugars, and organic labeling.

Orange Avocado Dressing

Blend 1 avocado with the juice of 2 oranges.

Supposedly the avocado was first eaten in 291 B.C. in Mexico by a Mayan princess who believed it held mystical and magical powers.
"The Ripe Stuff" by Kathy Farrell-Kingsley, *Vegetarian Times, March 1999*

Slaws

Slaws can be made from any sturdy vegetable-one that can be finely grated and hold firm when dressed. Some kids seem to be better able to eat slaws than leaves. To make a great slaw make combos from the following raw vegetables, grate them finely by pulsing them in the food processor then dress with the kids' favorite dressings or just lemon juice, maple syrup and olive or flax oil! Fresh herbs make a nice addition to slaws along with sunflower and pumpkin seeds.

Broccoli
Kohlrabi
Cauliflower
Carrots
Onion
Cabbages
Bell peppers
Turnips
Acorn squash
Butternut squash

Hummole

16 ozs. cooked chickpeas

1 avocado

3/4 of a jalapeno (optional)

1 clove garlic

Juice of 1 lemon

Blend all in the food processor 'til creamy.
Makes a great veggie dip!

Mexican Dip

1 can vegetarian refried beans, blended with 4 Tbs salsa

2 avocados, blended with juice of 1 lime

Shredded romaine lettuce

Sliced black olives

Layer all ingredients on a plate and serve with organic blue corn chips and additional salsa.

Nappa Kale Slaw

1 head nappa cabbage

1 bunch kale

1 bunch green onions

1 red bell pepper

1 inch fresh ginger

2 cloves garlic

4 Tbsp flax oil

1 Tbsp powdered dulse

Juice of 1 lemon or lime

Finely chop all the vegetables in food processor and dress. This is easy to chew after grinding in the food processor. Let sit for a few hours before serving to break down a bit more.

Mediterranean Grain Salad
By Rhonda B.

Crisp bell peppers, red onion and tangy kalamata olives add texture and color to this refreshing salad.

> 1 cup quinoa
> 1/3 cup red wine vinegar
> 2 tsp extra virgin olive oil
> 1 medium clove garlic, minced
> 1 medium red bell pepper, chopped
> 1 medium yellow bell pepper, chopped
> 1/2 cup chopped cucumber
> 1/4 cup sliced kalamata olives
> 1/4 cup chopped red onion
> 1/4 cup chopped fresh parsley

Cook quinoa (1 cup quinoa in 2 cups water, bring to boil, reduce heat and cover and simmer 10-15 minutes. Grain appears translucent when cooked.)

Meanwhile, make dressing: In small bowl, whisk together vinegar, oil and garlic. Season to taste with Celtic Sea Salt and pepper. Set aside.

In large bowl, combine peppers, cucumber, olives, onion, and parsley. Mix well. Add dressing and toss to coat. Add quinoa, stir gently but thoroughly to combine. Serve warm or at room temperature or even chilled the next day.

Nutritionally, quinoa might be considered a supergrain—although it is not really a grain, but the seed of a leafy plant that's distantly related to spinach. Quinoa has excellent reserves of protein, and unlike other grains, is not missing the amino acid lysine, so the protein is more complete (a trait it shares with other "non-true" grains such as buckwheat and amaranth). The World Health Organization has rated the quality of protein in quinoa at least equivalent to that in milk. Quinoa offers more iron than other grains and contains high levels of potassium and riboflavin, as well as other B vitamins: B6, niacin, and thiamin. It is also a good source of magnesium, zinc, copper, and manganese, and has some folate (folic acid). Quinoa should be rinsed thoroughly before cooking to remove any powdery residue of saponin.

www.wholehealthmd.com

Cathy's Iron-Packed Blended Salad for Mom's
from Cathy R.

> Handfuls of kale, green leaf lettuce and spinach
> 1/4 of a beet plus its greens
> 10 pieces of broccoli
> 1/2 cup of raisins-soaked in water to cover 1 hour plus the water
> 1/4 cup of yellow squash

Blend all in the blender to desired consistency adding water or fresh carrot juice as needed.

Hallelujah Kids

Strawberry Lunch Parfait

2 cups strawberries, hulled and sliced
1 banana, peeled and sliced
1 orange, peeled and sectioned
1 cup pineapple, peeled, cored, and sliced
1 cup lowfat vanilla or lemon soy or rice yogurt
1/4 cup Kashi™ cereal
Mint sprigs, optional
Juice of 1 orange

In a bowl mix strawberries, banana, orange and pineapple. Pour fresh orange juice over fruit and toss. Refrigerate until chilled. Put half the fruit into six parfait glasses then top with a heaping tablespoon of yogurt. Add remaining fruit; top each parfait glass with remaining yogurt. Sprinkle each parfait with Kashi™ cereal and garnish with a mint sprig.

Couscous Salad

1 tsp turmeric
1 can (16 oz) chickpeas, drained
1 cup chopped oranges
1/4 cup lemon juice
1 tsp orange zest (grated orange peel)
Red leaf lettuce
1-1/2 cup couscous, whole wheat
1/2 cup red onions, chopped
1/2 cup golden raisins
2 tsp olive oil
1 tsp chives, fresh minced

Cook the couscous according to package directions. Transfer to a large bowl. Stir in the chickpeas, oranges, onions and raisins. In a small bowl, whisk together the lemon juice, oil, orange peel and chives. Pour over the salad and toss. Refrigerate at least one hour. Serve on plates lined with lettuce.

Avo Salsa

1 avocado, peeled, cored and chopped

1 large tomato, chopped

1/4 cup red onion, finely chopped

2 cloves garlic, minced

2 Tbsp fresh cilantro, finely chopped

Juice of 1 lime

1/2 tsp cumin seeds, ground

Mix all ingredients and serve with veggies or organic chips.

A green idea

It's sometimes hard to get my son to enjoy collard greens, kale, spinach or similar type greens, especially raw. Here a recipe that he likes:

I chop the greens in a food processor with the S blade or run them through our Norwalk juicer with the largest grid, so they are chopped fine (less chewing required!) but not mushy. Then I mix some cold pressed oil (flax, almond, sunflower, olive, hazelnut) with about half as much lemon juice and mix in with the chopped greens. I only mix in enough to barely moisten the greens rather than overload them. My son likes Celtic salt on this. I often add some green stevia, since children seem always to love something sweet tasting. A finely chopped apple or pear could be added for sweetness.

From Annette K.
Charlottesville, VA

Hallelujah Kids

Pineapple Pepper Salsa

2 cups pineapple, peeled, cored and sliced
1/2 cup red bell pepper, seeded and diced
1/4 cup green onions, sliced
1 Tbsp cilantro, chopped
1 Tbsp jalapeno pepper, seeded and chopped
1 Tbsp fresh lime juice

Combine all ingredients. Serve over salad, as a side salad, or with organic tortilla chips. Mango can be substituted for the pineapple or use half mango and half pineapple. I love this as a salad dressing.

Black Bean Chili

1 Tbsp olive oil
2 cloves garlic, minced
1 onion, chopped
1 large carrot, chopped
1 jalapeno pepper, seeded and minced
1 sweet green pepper, seeded and chopped
3 large tomatoes, chopped
2 16 oz. cans black beans
1 Tbsp chili powder
1 tsp ground cumin
1 tsp crumbled dried rosemary

Garnish:

1 cup grated cucumber

Cook garlic, onion, carrot, jalapeno pepper and green pepper, stirring often for about 5 minutes. Stir in tomatoes, beans, chili powder, cumin, rosemary; bring to a boil. Reduce heat and simmer, uncovered, for 20 minutes. Season with salt. Serve garnished with cucumber.

Snow Peas with Cashews
from *Healthy 4 Him, Recipes for HealThy Living*

1 Tbsp shoyu

1/2 tsp red pepper flakes

1 tsp maple syrup

1 Tbsp olive oil

1 lb snow peas, chopped

1/4 cup raw cashews

3 cloves garlic

1 Tbsp gingerroot, grated

2 green onions, chopped

1 Tbsp lemon juice

Mix all ingredients together and marinate several hours or overnight.

Applesauce Pie
from *Healthy 4 Him, Recipes for HealThy Living*

Applesauce:

12 apples, unpeeled or peeled

2 Tbsp psyllium hulls

2 cups dates, soaked 1/2 hour in water then drained

Blend Applesauce ingredients in the food processor.
Stir in psyllium.

Crust:

1/2 cup almonds

1/2 cup walnuts

1 cup dates

Process all ingredients in food processor until it holds together loosely but is somewhat sticky. Press into pie plate, fill and chill for one hour until set.

Hallelujah Kids

Sprout Party Salad
from Sarah B., 10

2 lbs of your favorite sprouts
2 apples, cored and shopped
1 cup raisins
2 green onions, finely chopped
1 bunch red grapes, halved
1 bunch green grapes, halved
1 stalk celery, finely chopped
1 pound pecans or walnuts, chopped
2 bunches parsley, finely chopped

Mix all ingredients and serve.

Special Salad
from Sarah B., 10

2 bunches of flat leaf parsley, processed in food processor
1 tomato, chopped well
2 large cucumbers or zucchini, chopped well
Green onions, finely chopped
2 garlic cloves, minced
1/4 cup fresh lemon juice
1/4 cup olive oil

Combine all ingredients. Eat it with a fork or use it as a dip with vegetables or organic chips.

Carob Nut Butter
from Julia B., 12

> 2 coffee grinders full of almonds
> 1 tsp carob powder
> 1 Tbsp honey
> 1/2 tsp vanilla

Grind almonds in coffee grinder. Put in a bowl; add remaining ingredients and stir. I like to eat this on an apple or a banana.

Nutty Fruit Tossed Salad
from Julia B., 12

Salad:

> Green leaf lettuce
> Pineapple, peeled, cored, and sliced
> Apple, cored and diced
> Banana, peeled and sliced
> Raisins
> Pecans or cashews
> Celery, sliced

Dressing:

Combine

> Juice of 2-3 oranges
> 1 Tbsp honey

You can substitute pineapple juice for the orange juice.

Hallelujah Kids

Garden Sandwiches
from Julia B., 12

Cabbage, torn off carefully into large leaves
Grated carrot
Grated squash
Raisins
Celery, sliced
Cucumber, sliced
Green onion, sliced
Pickles, sliced

Use the cabbage leaves for the bread. Then put on everything else you like. You can add almond butter or Veganaise™ or dehydrated garden burger also. Then roll it up and eat.

Garden Burger
from Julia B., 12

Almonds
Carrot pulp
Onion, diced

Grind almonds in Champion juicer using the blank screen add carrot pulp left over from juicing carrots and finely diced onion. Mix all together well. You can eat it as is or dehydrate into burgers.

According to the Rainforest Action Network, 55 square feet of tropical rainforest, an area the size of a small kitchen, are destroyed for the production of every fast-food hamburger made from rainforest beef. Life forms destroyed in the production of each fast-food hamburger made from rainforest beef: Members of 20-30 different plant species, 100 different insect species and dozens of bird, mammal, and reptile species.

Denslow and Padoch, *People of the Tropical Rainforest*

Blended Salad
By Allison B.

Fresh vegetables (whatever you have in the refrigerator)
Almond butter, raisins, hummus, etc., for flavor variety

Wash, peel, and cut up vegetables. We usually choose from a variety, limiting it to three or four vegetables each meal. The possibilities are endless: carrots, broccoli, squash, tomatoes, zucchini, celery, cucumber, green leaf lettuce, spinach, cauliflower, avocado, etc. Put veggies into food processor and blend until you reach the desired consistency (very fine for young children). You can also add the flavoring in the processor with the veggies or wait and mix in later. Thin with a little water if it is too thick.

Hallelujah Kids

Couscous Blend

Organic couscous
Vegetable broth
Onions and mushrooms, sautéed

Cook couscous according to package directions in vegetable broth instead of water. Sautée onions and mushrooms and combine with couscous.

Sautéed Onions and Mushrooms

Sweet onion, sliced thick
Mushrooms, sliced thick
Olive oil to thinly coat skillet or wok
Pinch of cayenne (optional)

Heat olive oil over medium high heat. Place onions and mushrooms in skillet or wok and cook, stirring often, until onions are translucent.

Cucumber Salad

4 tomatoes, chopped large
2 cucumbers, chopped large
1 red bell pepper, seeded and chopped large
2 green onions, chopped
1 Tbsp dried mint
Juice of 1 lemon
4 Tbsp olive oil
Dash of garlic powder
Dash of Celtic Sea Salt

Mix salad ingredients and chill one hour. Serve over hot lentils and rice topped with grilled onions.

Lentils and Rice with Cucumber Salad
Corbin's favorite dinner

>2 cups lentils, cooked to package directions
>
>2 cups Jasmine rice, cooked to package directions
>
>Sweet onions, sautéed in skillet with olive oil

Serve with Cucumber Salad.

Sweet Sweet Potatoes

>3 medium sweet potatoes
>
>3 Tbsp honey
>
>Zest from 1 orange
>
>2 Tbsp freshly squeezed orange juice

Heat about 1/4 inch of water in a pan over medium heat; add sweet potatoes, cover and cook about 8 to 10 minutes or just until tender, turning often. Drain. Combine honey, orange peel and juice; pour over sweet potatoes and continue to cook, tossing until sweet potatoes are thoroughly glazed with the mixture.

Sweet potatoes are a Native American plant that was the main source of nourishment for early homesteaders and for soldiers during the Revolutionary War.

Now the sweet potato is a prime candidate for farming in outer space. On space stations, potato plants could provide nutritious food, while producing oxygen and removing carbon dioxide from the air.

Tender Brussels Sprouts

>Brussels sprouts

Bring a pot of water to boil-enough water to cover sprouts. Cut off the bottom stem area just a little bit then peel off the outer leaves. Place Brussels sprouts in a pan and bring to a boil. Then cover and simmer for 10 minutes until fork tender.

Hallelujah Kids

Brussels Sprouts were named after the capital of Belgium where it is thought that they were first cultivated. They are also one of the few vegetables to have originated in northern Europe. They were first introduced to France and England in the nineteenth century where they continue to be a popular food. French settlers who settled in Louisiana introduced them to America.

Brussels sprouts look like miniature heads of cabbage. They are similar to cabbage in taste, but they are slightly milder in flavor and denser in texture. Brussels sprouts and cabbage are members of the cruciferous vegetable family. These vegetables contain significant amounts of the antioxidants vitamin C and beta-carotene (vitamin A), and nitrogen compounds called indoles which may reduce the risk of certain cancers.

Brussels sprouts are a good source of vegetable protein, because 31 percent of the calories come from protein.

Pasta & Veggie Stew

1 bag (16 oz) small whole wheat pasta shells
1 can (32oz) tomato juice
2 cups water or vegetable broth
1 can (28 oz) diced tomatoes
1 cup frozen corn
1 cup frozen peas
1 cup frozen green beans
1 cup carrots, chopped
1/2 cup celery, chopped
1 onion, chopped
2 Tbsp Italian seasoning
1 clove garlic, pressed

Combine all ingredients in a large pot and simmer for one hour or more.

Vegetable Lo-Mein

8 oz udon noodles or Chinese wheat noodles

1 Tbsp olive oil

2 tsp dark sesame oil, divided

1 bag (8 oz) shredded cabbage and carrots

1 cup fresh green beans, trimmed and cut in half or frozen green beans

1 can (15 oz) cut baby corn, drained, reserve liquid

2 to 3 scallions cut into 1-inch segments

Vegetable stock or water, as needed

Natural low-sodium soy sauce to taste

Cook the noodles in plenty of rapidly simmering water until al dente, then drain. Meanwhile, heat the olive oil and 1 teaspoon of the sesame oil in a skillet or wok. Add the coleslaw, green beans, and 1/4 cup of the liquid from the baby corn. Cover and steam for 5 minutes.

Add the baby corn and scallions and stir-fry over medium-high heat for 5 minutes or until the vegetables are all just tender-crisp, adding just enough liquid from the baby corn to keep the bottom of the pan moist.

Combine the cooked noodles with the vegetables in a serving bowl and toss together. Add the remaining teaspoon of sesame oil, then season with soy sauce and grind in pepper to taste. Serve at once.

Baby Bok Choy Salad

6 heads baby bok choy, sliced

2 cups mung bean sprouts

2 cups snow peas, sliced

1 mango, chopped

1 cup wild rice, sprouted or cooked according to package directions

Juice of 2 limes

Pinch of garlic and/or cayenne (optional)

Toss all and marinade 2 hours or more. Even better the next day!

Hallelujah Kids

Quinoa and Edamame

1 package (8 oz) frozen shelled edamame beans

Cook according to package directions.

2 cups quinoa

4 cups water or vegetable broth

Bring to a boil then simmer 15-20 minutes until water is absorbed and quinoa is tender.

1 large carrot, finely chopped

2 stalks celery, finely chopped

1 onion, finely chopped

1 red bell pepper, seeded and finely chopped

3 cloves garlic

1 Tbsp Italian herbs

2 Tbsp olive oil

Pine nuts or sliced almonds for garnish

Saute vegetables until tender.

Add vegetables and edamame to quinoa and top with pine nuts or sliced almonds.

Bean Salad

2 cans organic chickpeas

1 can organic kidney beans

1 can organic butter beans

1 can organic peas

1 can organic green beans

1 sweet onion, sliced thin

4 Tbsp maple syrup

1/4 cup raw apple cider vinegar

1/2 tsp Celtic Sea Salt

Rinse and drain beans, any combination you like. Combine all ingredients marinade in the refrigerator for an hour or more.

Green Potato Salad

> 1 pound very small red potatoes
> 1 ripe avocado, peeled, cored and diced
> 1 small red onion, diced
> Lettuce leaves
> Minced parsley for garnish (optional)

Boil and drain potatoes. Let potatoes cool, cut into bite sized pieces and toss with the dressing, recipe below. Stir in diced avocado and onion. Serve over lettuce leaves, topped with minced fresh parsley.

Dressing:

> 1/2 a ripe avocado, peeled and cored
> 4 Tbsp flax oil
> 2 Tbsp lemon juice
> Dash hot sauce (optional)
> 1 clove garlic, pressed
> Dash Celtic Sea Salt

Blend all ingredients in food processor until creamy and serve over salad.

Raw Cranberry Salad
Trish M., Health Minister[SM]

> 1 pound bag of raw cranberries
> 1 large orange
> 1 large apple, cored
> 1/2 cup walnuts, crushed
> 2/2 cup raw unfiltered honey

Process everything but the nuts in food processor to a chunky applesauce consistency. Add nuts and chill. This is nice for holiday meals.

Hallelujah Kids

Pesto Wraps

Pesto:

> 4-6 cups fresh basil (measure before chopping)
> Juice of 3-4 lemons
> 1 cup pine nuts
> 2 cloves garlic
> 4 Tbsp olive oil

Chop basil in food processor then add remaining ingredients.

Wraps:

> 10-15 whole wheat lavash or sprouted tortillas
> Chopped veggies, any kind
> Chopped greens, any kind

Spread pesto on wraps; fill with veggies and roll up to eat.

Pesto Stuffed Cherry Tomatoes

> Large cherry tomatoes

Pesto:

> 4-6 cups fresh basil (measure before chopping)
> Juice of 3-4 lemons
> 1 cup pine nuts
> 2 cloves garlic
> 4 Tbsp olive oil

Chop basil in food processor then add remaining ingredients. Scoop the insides out of large cherry tomatoes with a strawberry plucker or baby spoon. Fill with pesto.

Seventh grader on a perfect attendance streak, thanks to The Hallelujah Diet

I like the Hallelujah Diet because it keeps me smart, strong, and hardly ever sick. (Lydia is in seventh grade and has never missed a day of school.) I like that sometimes my friends come up to me and ask if what they're eating is healthy too! Even if they made fun of me, though, I wouldn't care. Some of my favorite lunch foods are natural peanut butter & jelly, mangos, homemade pizza, beans & rice, salad, grapefruit and carrots.

Lydia M., 13¡

Mangos and grapefruit are a favorite for this Hallelujah Kid

I like Mom's pizza and desserts and spaghetti. My favorite lunch foods are natural peanut butter and jelly on a tortilla, Mom's pizza salad, mangos and grapefruit. I am hardly ever sick.

Alyssa M., 9 ¡

Mom and Health Minister Trish adds, Lydia and Alyssa didn't always enjoy carrot juice, BarleyMax and Udo's Oil but they don't fight me. They are wise enough to know it works.

Alyssa and Lydia

Hallelujah Kids

Pizza Salad
from Trish M., Health Minister[SM]

Crust Recipe:

>1 cup whole wheat bread flour
>
>1 cup whole grain spelt flour
>
>1 tsp yeast
>
>1 Tbsp olive oil
>
>1/2 cup warm distilled water
>
>Cornmeal
>
>2-3 cloves garlic
>
>1 tsp olive oil
>
>Sesame seeds, optional
>
>Pinch of dry oregano, optional

Place the first five ingredients in a bread maker (follow bread machine instructions for pizza dough) or in a bowl to knead by hand. When dough is done, oil and dust a 14" pan with cornmeal. Roll out the dough onto the pan. Mince garlic and mix with 1 tsp olive oil. Spread over the dough. Sprinkle with sesame seeds and dry oregano if desired. Bake at 350 degrees for 15-20 minutes. Cool slightly.

Salad:

Combine lettuce, chopped olives, mushrooms, artichoke hearts, or any other vegetable and pour on your favorite dressing.

Cut pizza crust into triangles and top with salad.

Green Beans and Corn on the Cob with Tomatoes

Cook a big pot of fresh picked green beans and another of fresh picked corn-on-the-cob. Slice some fresh picked-tomatoes and you have dinner!

Flat Tacos
from Trish M., Health Minister[SM]

      Small corn tortillas,
             placed in 300 degree oven for a few minutes until crisp
      Mashed pinto beans or canned organic refried beans
      Lettuce, shredded
      Sweet onion, chopped
      Olives, chopped
      Tomatoes, chopped
      Raw corn
      Avocado or guacamole
      Raw salsa
      Any variety of raw veggies, chopped

Put out the ingredients and let the kids build layer their tacos themselves. That's half the fun! You can even pack this for lunch leaving the tortillas in a separate baggie.

Bean Burritos

      Whole wheat burrito wraps
      Pinto beans cooked and blended with salsa or organic
             vegetarian canned refried beans, heated
      Tomatoes, diced
      Olives, sliced
      Sweet onion, diced
      Romaine lettuce, shredded
      Salsa, fresh or organic bottled
      Non-dairy sour cream (optional)

Layer beans and vegetables in the center of each wrap; top with sour cream; fold into burritos.

Hallelujah Kids

Taco Salad

Romaine lettuce, shredded
Tomatoes, diced
Sweet onions, diced
Olives, sliced
Avocado slices or Guacamole
Pinto beans, cooked and blended with salsa
      or organic refried beans, heated
Cooked brown rice
Salsa for dressing
Non-dairy sour cream (optional)

Make a salad with romaine lettuce and veggies; top with remaining ingredients.

From the royal tombs of ancient Egypt to the Old Testament cultivation, preparation, and consumption of beans are recognized. The lima and pinto bean were cultivated for the first time in the very earliest Mexican and Peruvian civilizations more than 5,000 years ago, being popular in both the Aztec and Inca cultures.

The United States is by far the world leader in dry bean production. Each year, U.S. farmers plant from 1.5 to 1.7 million acres of edible dry beans. And while Americans are the chief consumers of these beans, 40 percent are shipped to international markets in more than 100 different countries around the globe.

CDC's 5 A Day Program

In some parts of Europe, children afflicted with measles, mumps, or chickenpox are sponged with water in which peas have been boiled. This apparently seems to keep them from itching so much and from forming permanent pit marks in the skin.

John Heinerman's New Encyclopedia of Fruits & Vegetables

Creamy Beans and Peas

1/2 cup dried yellow split peas
3 cups water
1 tsp turmeric
1 can (15 oz) black beans
1 can (15 oz) kidney beans
2 Tbsp olive oil
1 sweet onion, chopped
1 clove garlic, minced
1 tsp fresh ginger, minced
1 tsp cumin
1/2 tsp coriander
1/2 tsp cayenne
1/4 tsp cardamom
1 can (14.5 oz) diced tomatoes

Boil the split peas for one minute, add the turmeric and simmer for additional 20 minutes. Add the beans and simmer another 20 minutes. Heat the oil in a skillet, add the onions and cook for 5 minutes. Add the garlic, ginger, remaining spices and tomatoes. Add the skillet contents to the big pot and heat through. Note: when using canned beans, organic and salt-free are best.

Hummus Sandwiches

Sprouted grain bread
Your favorite hummus
Lettuce leaves
Slices of tomato
Slices of onion

Spread the hummus on bread and top with lettuce, tomato and onion.

Hallelujah Kids

Pita Bread with Hummus, Cucumbers & Tomatoes

Whole wheat pita bread
Your favorite hummus
Cucumber slices
Tomato slices

Fill pita pockets with hummus and veggies.

Tomatoes were once called love apples, because of a superstition that eating a tomato would make one fall in love!

Cabbage Roll Stew

1 can (28 oz) tomatoes
3 Tbsp honey
Juice of 1 lemon
1 onion, chopped
1/2 tsp celery seeds
1/2 tsp allspice
1 cup water or vegetable broth
1 head cabbage, chopped
1 cup cooked brown rice
1 can kidney beans, drained
1 large onion, finely chopped
1/2 cup parsley
1 Tbsp sage

Combine all in a large pot and heat through.

Chickpeas & Couscous

1 small onion, chopped
3 carrots, chopped
1 can (15 oz) garbanzo beans, drained
1 cup vegetable broth
3 cloves garlic, pressed
1/4 tsp nutmeg
1/4 tsp cinnamon
1 tsp cumin
1/2 tsp turmeric
1/4 tsp cayenne pepper
1-1/2 cups couscous

Simmer all but couscous for 20 minutes. Add couscous and cook 15 minutes more.

Potato Cabbage Soup

A kid favorite at our house! Serve this after a big bowl of raw veggies.

3 pounds Yukon gold potatoes, cubed
1 cup pearl onions or big chopped onions
1 head cabbage, sliced thick
1 Tbsp vegetable broth mix
4 cups water

Boil water with vegetable broth mix and potatoes until fork tender. Add onions and cabbage; cook until cabbage is done, about 20 minutes. Stir to smash a bit of the potatoes to make the soup creamy.

Hallelujah Kids

Corn Chowder

 2 bags (16 oz) frozen corn, thawed
 2 cups rice or almond milk
 Potatoes, diced
 Onions, diced
 Celery, diced

Process corn and milk in blender or food processor until creamy. Add veggies; bring to boil then lower heat and simmer for 20 minutes until veggies are tender.

Chickpea & Spinach Stew
Another one of our favorites!

 2 Tbsp olive oil
 1 onion, chopped
 2 cloves garlic, pressed
 2 cans (18 oz) chickpeas
 1 can (28 oz) diced tomatoes or 4 fresh tomatoes, diced
 1 pound spinach
 1 tsp cumin
 1 Tbsp Italian herb seasoning
 1/2 tsp Celtic Sea Salt (optional)
 1 Tbsp honey

In a large pot, cook onions and garlic in oil for 5 minutes. Add chickpeas and tomatoes. Cover and simmer for 15 minutes. Put spinach on top, replace lid and simmer another 10 minutes stirring in the spinach as it wilts. Serve with cut veggies, pita bread and hummus. My two kids can eat the whole recipe in one night for their dinner meal (minus the bites Mom takes when fixing it!).

Corn-on-the-Cob

Ears of raw corn-on-the-cob

Let the kids peel, wash and eat!

Grilled Corn-on-the-Cob

When we go to barbecues, we always bring corn-on-the-cob. We eat a few raw while waiting for the rest to come off the grill!

Ears of raw corn, unshucked, soaked in water for 30 minutes. Lay whole unshucked ears of corn, uncovered, on the grill and cook for 15 minutes. Then shuck (careful, it's hot) and eat.

Did you know...?

- Corn provides nearly 20 percent of the world's food calories.

- Corn is grown in Africa more widely than any other crop.

- The United States grows 45 percent of the world's corn, much of which is processed into animal feed.

- A bushel of corn yields 2.5 gallons of ethanol: a renewable fuel used instead of lead to raise gasoline octane levels.

- Corn is sweetest eaten young, fresh and raw!

Hallelujah Kids

Three-Bean Chili

1/2 cup water or vegetable broth or wine

1 medium onion, chopped

2 clove garlic, minced

1 medium carrot, chopped

7 cups water

1/3 cup tomato puree

2 cups brown lentils

1 green bell pepper, seeded and chopped

1 yellow or red bell pepper, seeded and chopped

2-1/2 cups cooked or canned dark kidney beans, drained and rinsed

1 cup cooked or canned pinto beans, drained and rinsed

2 cups chopped fresh or canned tomatoes with juice

1 Tbsp chili powder

1 Tbsp ground cumin

1/4 tsp cayenne pepper

1/4 tsp black pepper

Heat the water or broth in a large heavy soup pot over medium heat. Add the onion, garlic, and carrot. Cook and stir over medium heat about 5 minutes. Add more liquid if necessary. Add 7 cups water, tomato puree, lentils, green pepper, yellow pepper, red kidney beans, pinto beans, tomatoes, chili powder, cumin, cayenne pepper, and black pepper. Bring to a boil. Reduce heat, cover, and simmer for 45 minutes until lentils are tender, adding more water if necessary.

The fiery characteristic in chile peppers is due to a very potent chemical called capsaicin. In general, the smaller the chile, the bigger the thermonuclear detonation it's capable of delivering.
John Heinerman's New Encyclopedia of Fruits & Vegetables

Chili Lime Onions

10 green pablano or mild chilis, cut into thin strips
4 big white onions, ringed
4 limes, juiced
1/2 tsp oregano
Dash of Celtic Sea Salt
2 Tbsp maple syrup

Mix all and marinate 2 hours. This makes a nice dinner simply served over a bed of romaine lettuce or as a side dish to other Mexican dishes.

Broccoli Almond Slaw

Dressing:

1/4 cup raw almond butter
Pinch unrefined Celtic Sea Salt
1 clove garlic
Juice of 2 limes
Water to thin

Salad:

1/4 cup fresh cilantro
1/4 cup fresh mint
4 green onions, minced
1 carrot, shaved
1 head broccoli, finely chopped
1 red bell pepper, seeded and thinly sliced

Whisk dressing and toss with salad. Finely chopping the broccoli makes it easy for kids to eat a lot of it!

Hallelujah Kids

Pasta Soup

2 carrots, diced

1 onion, diced

2 stalks celery, diced

2 Tbsp olive oil

2 cups mixed small beans and lentils

1 can (28 oz) diced tomatoes

2 boxes vegetable broth, low sodium

2 Tbsp dried thyme, rosemary, parsley mix

1 cup small pasta noodles—any shape

Sauté the carrots, onions and celery in olive oil. Add broth, beans, tomatoes, and herbs. Cover and simmer 3 hours. Add pasta and cook uncovered 10-15 minutes more.

Old Fashioned Vegetable Soup

1-1/2 gallons organic tomato juice

1 can (28 oz) diced tomatoes

2 Tbsp vegetable broth mix

4 cups water

1 bag (16 oz) frozen corn

1 bag (16 oz) frozen green beans

1 bag (16 oz) frozen peas

1 bag (12 oz) frozen edamame beans

1 bag (16 oz) frozen broccoli

4 large carrots, sliced

4 stalks celery-sliced

1 onion, diced

2 Tbsp celery seed

2 Tbsp dried oregano

2 Tbsp dried parsley

Put all ingredients into a large pot; bring to a boil, then cover and simmer 4 hours or more.

Man designed the automobile engine to run on a certain octane of gasoline. If we put a low grade fuel in the gas tank of our automobile, it will ping and knock. If we put sugar in the gas tank of our automobile, it will destroy the engine. So we are careful to put only the proper octane of fuel, without contaminants, into our automobile so that it will run properly.

Well, God created man, and He designed man to run on only one kind of fuel . . . PLANT FOOD! Man's body is a living organism, made of living cells, which require living food in order to be properly nourished and function well. When we put more cooked food than living food into our body, the body starts to break down. It begins in the very young with colic, rashes, colds, earaches, upset stomachs, swollen glands and tonsils. As the child grows older, there may be tooth decay, pimples, the need for eye glasses, etc. Then as we enter adult life there is arthritis, hypoglycemia, heart attacks, strokes, diabetes and cancers. All this and a multitude of other diseases are unnecessary and are nothing but the result of improper diet and lifestyle!

Rev. George Malkmus www.hacres.com

"Race car drivers need not know the chemical formula for their fuel. Kids should not have to be chemists in order to eat well, just be able to recognize premium fuel choices from regular."
Dr. Doug Graham

Gabe S. age 3
Son of Jerrod & Nikki,
Health Ministers[SM]

Hallelujah Kids

Cindy's Lunch Treats
from Cindy P.

1 or 2 frozen bananas
Handful of berries, fresh or frozen
Handful of raw almonds
2 dates

Run banana and berries through the Champion Juicer with the blank screen in place. Grind almonds and dates in food processor.

Put banana ice cream into a small plastic container and top with almond/date crumbles. Freeze. Put in lunch box in the morning as an ice pack then it will be half-thawed at lunchtime!

Split Pea Soup

1 pound split green peas
2 quarts water
1 large onion, diced
4 large carrots, shredded
1 large kohlrabi, shredded
3 cloves garlic
4 Tbsp vegetable broth mix

Combine all ingredients in a large pot; bring to a boil then cover and simmer for an hour or more.

Val's Cucumber Soup
from Val R.

4 organic cucumbers, diced
1 mango, peeled and diced
Juice of 1 lime

Blend all in food processor or blender.

"Cool as a cucumber" isn't just a catchy phrase. The inner temperature of a cucumber can be up to 20 degrees cooler than the outside air. No wonder cucumbers are such a summertime favorite!

Cucumbers were believed to have originated in India and spread through Greece and Italy. They made their way into North America agriculture by the mid-16 century. Cool and moist due to their high water content. "Cukes" belong to the same family as pumpkins, zucchini, watermelon and other squashes.

CDC's 5 A Day Program

Whole Wheat Cornbread

1-1/4 cup whole wheat pastry flour

3/4 cup cornmeal

1/4 cup honey

2 tsp baking powder

1 cup rice milk

1/4 cup walnut oil

2 Tbsp ground flax seeds

Combine all ingredients and bake at 400 degrees for 25 minutes in a stone or nonstick pan.

Hummus

1 - 16 oz can organic chickpeas/garbanzo beans

2 T raw tahini

Juice of 1 lemon

1 clove garlic (option)

Pinch of Celtic Sea Salt (optional)

Water to thin if necessary

Blend in the food processor adding water as it blends.

Hallelujah Kids

Lentils and Pasta Italiana
from Rhonda B.

1 pound cooked pasta (corkscrews or twists are good)
2 cups cooked lentils (I cook up a bag of them and store them
in the freezer—2 C to a freezer bag—they thaw quickly)

While pasta is cooking, in large stock pan sauté in olive oil until translucent:

1 large yellow onion, sliced
2 cloves garlic, pressed, minced, or sliced

Combine all ingredients then garnish with fresh basil leaves.

> Lentils are "fast-food" legumes—no need to pre-soak—just rinse
> and cook, about 10-20 minutes depending on size.

Middle East Pinto Soup
Rhonda B.

1 pound pinto beans
3 vegan bouillion cubes
5 potatoes, cubed

Cook pinto beans in water to cover with bouillion cubes. Add potatoes and simmer
until cooked.

Sautée in olive oil:

2 cups chopped yellow onion
3-4 leaves of Swiss chard, chopped

Add the onions and Swiss chard to the beans and potatoes.
Add:

1-2 Tbsp parsley flakes or a bunch of fresh, chopped parsley
Celtic Sea Salt (to taste)

Olive oil is a fruit-juice. Olive oil is cold pressed olive juice and olives are a fruit. That's why it's so healthy and is used in the finest cuisines all over the world. Cold pressed means that the olives are picked and squeezed and are not boiled before squeezing.

Cauliflower and Pasta
from Guida S.

> 1 lb. whole grain pasta
> 1 head cauliflower

Cook pasta. While it is underway, wash and cut up one head of cauliflower into pieces. Steam the cauliflower.

While the pasta and cauliflower are going, mix in a large bowl:

Sauce:

> 8 oz non-dairy sour cream
> 1/2 Tbsp poppy seeds
> 1-2 tsp horseradish, to taste
> Celtic Sea Salt, to taste

Drain pasta. When cauliflower is cooked until tender, toss it into the sauce and mash it a bit with a handheld pastry blender. It should be "chunky." Pour it over the pasta. Serve with additional horseradish.

Hallelujah Kids

Lentil Soup
from Rhonda B.

> 2 Tbsp olive oil
> 3 or 4 leaves Swiss chard, chopped fine
> (OR you can substitute with 1 bunch (3/4 C) fresh parsley, chopped)
> 1 large yellow onion, chopped
> 2 cloves garlic, peeled and pressed or chopped fine

In large soup pan, sautée in 2 Tbsp olive oil just until tender.

Add:

> 6 cups water and 2 vegan bouillon cubes
> 1-1/2 cup lentils (rinse them in a colander first, and pick out any little sticks and things)

Bring to boil, and simmer 20 minutes.

Add:

> 6 potatoes, peeled and diced
> 1 Tbsp dried parsley (if you used the Swiss chard earlier)
> 1 tsp mint
> Celtic Sea Salt (to taste)

Simmer 10 minutes until the potatoes are cooked.

Add:

> 2 Tbsp lemon juice and enjoy!

Garbanzo/Walnut Patties

1/2 cup cooked garbanzo beans/chickpeas

1/2 cup water

1 cup rolled oats, uncooked

1 cup walnuts, chopped

1 onion, minced

4 Tbsp rice or almond milk

1 tsp dried sage

1 tsp celery seed

Blend the beans and water until creamy. Stir in the remaining ingredients. Form patties with your hands and pan-fry in non-stick skillet or small amount of olive oil.

Garbanzos and Couscous

1 small onion, chopped

3 carrots, chopped

1 can (14-1/2 oz) diced tomatoes

1 can (15 oz) garbanzo beans, drained

1 cup vegetable broth

3 cloves garlic, pressed

1/4 tsp ground nutmeg

1/4 tsp ground cinnamon

1 tsp ground cumin

1/2 tsp turmeric

1/4 tsp cayenne pepper

1-1/2 cups cooked couscous

Combine all ingredients except couscous in a pot. Bring to a boil, then reduce heat and simmer, covered, for an hour. Add cooked couscous during last 15 minutes of cooking.

Hallelujah Kids

Lentil Stew

1 pound lentils
1/2 cup brown rice
1 cup carrots, chopped
1 cup bell pepper, seeded and chopped
1 cup celery, chopped
1 onion, chopped
2 tomatoes, chopped
1 cup tomato sauce
1 Tbsp molasses
1-1/2 tsp salt
1 tsp dried basil
1/2 tsp dried thyme
1 clove garlic, pressed
1 Tbsp lemon juice

Wash and sort lentils. Place in large pot, cover with water by 2-3 inches. Bring to a boil then reduce heat and simmer, covered, for 30 minutes. Add brown rice and simmer 30 more minutes. Add remaining ingredients except for lemon juice and simmer another one hour. Add lemon juice just before serving. May also be made in a crock-pot; add water to a level 2-3 inches above lentils and cook for 5 hours on high.

Spicy Almonds

2 cups raw almonds - water to cover
1 cup your favorite hot sauce

Soak almonds for 4 hours in water to cover. Drain water then stir in hot sauce. Soak 15 minutes in hot sauce. Dehydrate in dehydrator over night the til crispy.

> "An inventory of the household goods of the Queen of France in 1372 listed only twenty pounds of sugar but included over five hundred pounds of almonds."
> *John Heinerman, Encyclopedia of Nuts, Berries and Seeds*

```
Hallelujah Twins feeling great!

    Josh & Emily are 4th grade homeschoolers enjoying better
health and quality of life.
    Josh's favorite foods are steamed broccoli along with a
salad of romaine lettuce, tomatoes, cucumbers, celery, car-
rots and turnips without dressing. In his lunchbox he packs
salad in a baggie, cut veggies, apples, rice cakes, veggie
pita wraps and dried fruits.
    He plays basketball, soccer and
skateboards. His favorite Bible verse is
John 3:16!
    Emily enjoys making her favorite
recipes below for Salad Suppers hosted
by Health Ministers, Charlie & Carol.
She also likes to go jogging, play soc-
cer, play in her treehouse and partici-
pate in hobbies of stamp collecting,
sewing, reading and rollerblading. Her
favorite Bible verse is Psalm 18:1-2!

                           Josh and Emily M.
                           10 year old twins
```

Veggie Pitas
from Josh & Emily

>   Whole wheat pita bread
>   Alfalfa sprouts
>   Romaine lettuce
>   Carrots, shredded
>   Celery, diced

Pita Pizzas
from Josh & Emily

>   Whole wheat pita bread
>   Organic pasta sauce
>   Rice cheese

Cut pitas in half and lay on a cookie sheet. Spread with pasta sauce then sprinkle with cheese. Bake at 350 degrees for 10 minutes.

Hallelujah Kids

Cranberry Sauce *from Josh & Emily*

   1 bag raw cranberries

   1-12 oz frozen orange juice concentrate, thawed

   12 red delicious apples

   Stevia (optional)

Quarter and seed apples. Blend in the blender til saucy.

Carob Smoothies *from Josh & Emily*

   4 Tbsp carob powder

   1 cup water

   4 dates, pitted

   2 Tbsp raw almonds

   7 frozen bananas

Blend in blender.

Chocolate Milk *from Prudy M., Health Minister*[SM] *for Josh & Emily*

   3 cups water

   1 cup soaked sunflower seeds

   3 Tbsp carob powder

   3 squirts of stevia liquid

Blend in blender. Strain and serve chilled.

Cabbage Delight *from Prudy M., Health Minister*[SM] *for Josh & Emily*

   1 head purple cabbage, shredded

   2-1/2 apples, peeled, cored and chopped small

   2 Tbsp red onion, chopped

Dressing:

   1/3 cup raw apple cider vinegar

   1/3 cup olive oil

   2 Tbsp maple syrup

   1 tsp Celtic Sea Salt (optional)

   3 Tbsp curly parsley, chopped

   2 Tbsp cilantro, chopped

Shake dressing and pour over salad.

Snacks and Desserts

Pumpkin Cookies
from Vandy S.

2 cups whole wheat flour

1 cup rolled oats

1/4 cup ground flax seeds

1 tsp non-aluminum baking powder

1 tsp cinnamon

1/2 tsp Celtic Sea Salt

1 cup melted organic butter

1 cup amber agave nectar

2 Tbsp ground flax seed mixed with 1/4 cup water

1 cup pumpkin puree

3/4 cup chopped walnuts (optional)

Preheat oven to 350 degrees. Blend the dry ingredients together. Blend the wet ingredients together separately. Combine dry ingredients into the wet ones slowly. Stir in nuts. Line baking sheets with parchment paper. Drop dough by the tablespoon or ice cream scooper onto sheets. Bake 7-9 minutes til golden, sheen is gone from top of cookies and they spring back when pressed lightly. Cool 1-2 minutes on the cookie sheets then move to wire racks to cool.

Americans, who comprise only 5 percent of the world's population, account for a whopping 33 percent of total global sugar consumption—over 10 million tons annually.
Toronto Sun 1-25-04

Corbin's Banana Mango Parfait
When dessert can become dinner!

Crumbles:

> 2 cups almonds
> 1 cup dates

Grind almonds and dates in food processor.

Pudding:

> 10 ripe bananas
> 4 mangos
> Juice and zest of 3 lemons

Blend pudding ingredients into a pudding-like consistency. Alternate layers of pudding and crumbles in parfait glasses. Top with sliced strawberries, sliced kiwis and/or blueberries. Sprinkle with coconut.

"Nuts and seeds are wonderful foods that can help ensure that your children develop healthy bodies and minds. In fact, one important key to your children's ongoing good health is to eliminate dairy products (low-nutrient foods, containing high saturated fat) from their diets and make raw nuts and seeds (high-nutrient foods, containing unsaturated fat) their major source of fat."

Dr. Joel Fuhrman www.drfuhrman.com

Seed Bars

To make seed bars, put dry ingredients in a large bowl. Heat just a few tablespoons of honey and pour over dry mix. Stir well until coated. If you put in too much honey, add more seeds! You are looking for a pretty dry consistency. Press into a stone pan or a cookie sheet to set in the fridge.

Combo #1

Sesame seeds
Sunflower seeds
Flax seeds
Date pieces (with oat flour)
Honey
Shelled hempseeds

Combo #2

Sunflower seeds
Honey
Shelled hempseeds
Flax seeds
Pumpkin seeds

Combo #3

Sunflower seeds
Honey
Sesame seeds
Flax seeds
Pumpkin seeds
Raisins
Almonds

Hallelujah Kids

Spicy Chili Flax Crackers

4 cups flaxseeds
2 cups water

Blend:

2 cups Sunflower seeds
Half an onion, chopped
1/4 cup shredded unsulphured coconut
1 tsp ground ginger
4 cloves garlic
2 Tbsp red chili powder
1/2 tsp Celtic Sea Salt
1 Tbsp nama shoyu
1/2 - 1 tsp cayenne
1 tsp liquid smoke
1/2 tsp mustard seed
1 tsp cumin seeds

Soak flaxseeds in water. Blend remaining ingredients and pour into flax goo. Let sit 10 minutes. Pour out onto teflex dehydrator sheets and spread to 1/4 inch thickness. Dehydrate until they can be turned; turn and continue drying until crispy. to make less spicy just leave out some spices.

Brownies

2 cups cashews, soaked 30 minutes and drained
2 Tbsp cocoa powder or carob powder
1/2 cup almonds
1/2 cup honey or agave nectar
4 Tbsp chopped hazelnuts
Water to blend

Blend all ingredients; the consistency will be thick. Spread mixture onto teflex dehydrator sheets. Dry, turning after 12 hours (peel off teflex sheet), until chewy brownie consistency, about 24 hours total.

Raw "Chocolate" Cake
from Allison B.

Crust:

> 5 cups ground raw nuts
>
> 3 cups raisins
>
> 3 Tbsp raw carob powder
>
> 1 tsp vanilla
>
> 1/2 tsp Celtic Sea Salt

Combine all ingredients in bowl of food processor and blend using the S blade.

Topping:

> 1/2 cup water
>
> 1 cup raw tahini
>
> 6 Tbsp raw honey
>
> 3 Tbsp carob powder
>
> 1 tsp vanilla

Combine all ingredients in bowl of food processor and blend using the S blade. Spread topping evenly over crust. Decorate with fruits, berries, and nuts. Chill.

If you have any topping left over, roll bananas in it, then roll the bananas in chopped pecans and freeze for a yummy treat.

Celery & Dates
from Dave R.

> Celery boats, cut in 2-inch lengths
>
> Dates, sliced to fit inside the length of celery

Lay dates into celery boats.

The unique taste of the Medjool so captivated royalty that they hoarded the fruit and only they and their families knew of its delicate, but satisfying taste.

At the turn of the century, a rare disease killed the beautiful palms of Morocco and only one Medjool producing oasis survived the attack.

Thanks to a man named Carrifi, who defied his countrymen by relocating eleven healthy palms, the Medjool escaped total extinction.

Eventually the Medjool, characterized by its high sugar content and meaty plumpness, thrived once again. And gradually new areas were found that could produce this most delicate of fruits.

One such area is Southern California where the majestic Medjool producing palms sprinkle the banks of the Colorado River. The fruit which was once reserved for royalty has become the most widely chosen date in the world.

The time and care required to ensure the uniqueness of the Medjool remains amazingly similar to that displayed in ancient Morocco. Medjool growers, to ensure huge, plump dates, thin out about 90% of the dates on each bloom to allow the remaining 20 percent to reach their maximum size. It takes one man all day to thin four trees.

When it's time to harvest, experienced men ascent the forty foot palms and carefully pick the Medjools by hand. Machines are also forbidden in the packaging of Medjools for fear of damaging this precious fruit. The Medjool date, once a delicacy known only to royalty, is now the most popular date in the world. Enjoy!

BARD VALLEY MEDJOOL DATE GROWERS ASSOCIATION

Coconut Dates

Cut dates in half, length-wise, remove the pits, then press the sticky side into unsweetened, unsulphured, shredded coconut.

Fig Snacks

Turkish figs
Pecans

Take a bite of each and let the flavors blend in your mouth.

It may surprise you to know that when you eat a half-cup of figs you get as much calcium as when you drink a half-cup of milk.
Valley Figs

Watermelon Ice

1 cup frozen watermelon
1 cup fresh watermelon

Blend together in the food processor.

One would have to eat approximately 500 lbs of grapefruit, 100 lbs of watermelon, 100 pounds of almonds, 35 pounds of dates, and 25 pounds of bananas-all at the same meal— to equal the sodium in two bologna sandwiches!
Diet by Design, Author Unknown

Hallelujah Kids

Fruit Pie
from Carol S., Health Minister[SM]

This makes a great birthday party treat. You can change the fruit and amount of honey in this recipe to your taste. If you use raw, unfiltered honey, you have a raw spread or a pie filling. I use it to make tiny tarts.

Filling:

> **2 cups fresh organic strawberries, hulled**
> **2 Tbsp raw, unfiltered honey**
> **2 Tbsp pure psyllium husk (add until proper consistency is reached)**

Blend in blender. Let set a few minutes.

Crust:

> **2 cups raw nuts (I like pecans)**
> **3-4 Tbsp pure maple syrup**
> **1 tsp pure vanilla**

Place nuts in the bowl of a food processor and, using the S blade, blend to a fine texture. Mix syrup and vanilla together and blend into nuts with a fork until nuts cling. Press into tart shells or pie plate. Cover with a layer of strawberries then fill with the filling.

Almond Butter & Honey Spread
from Corbin & Ryan W.

> **Apple wedges**
> **Raw almond butter**
> **Honey**

Mix equal amounts of honey and almond butter with a fork until creamy. Dip apple wedges.

Apples were brought to North America with Columbus in the 1490's, and moved to the western US with pioneers, John Chapman (alias Johnny Appleseed) and missionaries during the 1800's.

Maple Nut Bars
from Valerie D.

> 6 oz almonds
>
> 5 oz walnuts
>
> 4 oz pecans
>
> 3 oz macadamias
>
> 1/2 cup maple syrup
>
> 1/4 cup distilled water (more or less as needed)

Grind the nuts in food processor until fine, and with processor still running, pour in maple syrup. If the mixture is too thick or crumbly, slowly pour in water until mixture is smooth, but still thick. (You don't want to add too much water because that will add to the time it needs to dehydrate.) Using a two-tablespoon scoop, place portions of the mixture on teflex sheets (this made 32 portions divided between two sheets). Flatten each portion to about 1/4 inch and dehydrate 24-36 hours, depending on how firm you want them.

Walnuts contain the 'good' fat - polyunsaturated fat - that our bodies need. They are one of the few plant sources of Omega-3 fatty acids. High intake of this essential fatty acid has been associated with a lower risk of cardiovascular disease. Just one ounce of walnuts contains 2.57 grams of Omega-3s. They are an excellent plant source of protein, low in saturated fat, and have no cholesterol. Sealed and refrigerated, walnuts can be kept for up to a year.
SunOrganic Farm www.sunorganicfarm.com

Cherry Cheesecake

Crust:

> 2 cups raw almonds
> 1/2 cup pitted dates
> 1/4 cup grated coconut, unsulphured, unsweetened
> 1/2 tsp Celtic Sea Salt

Combine all ingredients in bowl of food processor and process using the S blade. Press into pie plate.

Filling:

> 4 cups raw cashews, soaked in water to cover 2 hours and drained
> 3/4 cup fresh lemon juice
> 2 bananas
> 1 tsp ground flax seeds
> 3/4 cup raw honey, at room temp
> 1 tsp vanilla

Place all ingredients in food processor and blend using the S blade until smooth and thick. Pour into crust.

Sauce:

> 2 cups fresh pitted cherries
> (or strawberries, or blueberries or raspberries, or blackberries)
> 1/2 cup pitted dates

Place ingredients in food processor blend using the S blade. Pour over pie. Top with sliced whatever berry you used and sprinkle with coconut. Set in the freezer for an hour or more. Serve frozen.

Cheesecake Variations

Carob:

    Add 3 Tbsp carob powder to filling.

    Top with icing made of carob powder and maple syrup.

Carob Mint:

    Add 3 Tbsp carob powder and 1/2 tsp peppermint extract or more to taste.

    Top with icing made of carob powder and maple syrup.

Pistachio:

    Substitute 2 cups raw pistachios for 2 cups cashews for filling.

    Replace half the lemon juice with lime juice.

The Queen of Sheba, who lived at the time of King Solomon in the southern part of ancient Arabia, held pistachio nuts in such high esteem that she demanded that all pistachios produced in her land be given to her and her court, and she hoarded the bulk of the crop for herself.

From Healthy Nuts by Gene Spiller, PhD

Mango:

    Replace 2 bananas with 1 big mango for filling.

    Top with icing made of 2 cups blended mango and 1/2 cup pitted dates.

Orange:

    Replace lemon juice with fresh orange juice for filling.

Mini-Cheesecakes:

    Press 1 tsp crust mixture into the bottom of paper cup lined mini-muffin pan.

    Fill with filling and add topping. Freeze. Pop out onto platter to serve.

Hallelujah Kids

Song of Songs Nut Cakes
From Food at the Time of the Bible by Miriam Vamosh

This is an ancient Egyptian recipe from 1600 B.C. discovered on an ostracon, a fragment (as of pottery) containing an inscription.

> 1 cup pitted dates
> 1/4 - 1/2 cup water
> 1 tsp cinnamon
> 1/4 tsp cardamom
> 1/2 cup chopped walnuts
> 1/2 cup chopped almonds
> Honey

In a food processor with the S blade, mix the dates to a paste with the water. Add the spices, walnuts and 1/4 cup almonds and mix well. Form into small balls, coat with honey and roll in remaining almonds.

Banana Chips and Carob Fudge
from Corbin W., 13

> Unsweetened, unsulphured banana chips for dipping

Fudge:

> 1/2 cup carob powder
> 1/2 cup raw almond butter
> Maple syrup to desired consistency

Combine all ingredients and mix well. Dip banana chips or spread the fudge on organic graham crackers. For a fruit dip, add water to the fudge to desired consistency.

Trail Mix

Trail mixes can be made with any combination of the following raw ingredients...

Almonds

Walnuts

Hazelnuts

Brazil nuts

Cashews

Pecans

Sunflower seeds

Pumpkin seeds

Raisins

Dates

> "The Brazil nut is blessed by the Amazon soil in the tropics, soil that is extremely rich in selenium. Selenium is a mineral with powerful antioxidant properties. It is essential to health and may help prevent some types of cancer."
> *Healthy Nuts* by Gene Spiller, PhD

Fruit & Nut Bars

1/2 cup dried unsulphured, unsweetened apricots

1 cup dates, pitted

1 cup dried unsulphured, unsweetened figs

3 Tbsp fresh orange juice

3/4 cup unsulphured, unsweetened shredded coconut

1/2 cup almonds, ground

Zest of 1 orange

Combine and process all ingredients in the bowl of food processor using the S blade. Press mix into 8-inch square pan. Chill for one hour then cut into bars. Store in the refrigerator. Top with extra coconut before serving.

Hallelujah Kids

Dates are perhaps the oldest tree crop cultivated by man. More than 5000 years ago this valuable tree helped sustain the desert and nomadic peoples of the Middle East and North Africa. Dates have been found in earthen jars in the tombs of Pharaohs and Kings, so placed to give them sustenance in their trip to the afterworld.
Western Date Ranches

Frozen Carob Bananas

Liquid honey
Carob powder
Walnuts or almonds, chopped fine
Bananas, ripe but firm
Wooden skewers

Skewer a banana. Gently roll banana in honey then carob powder then chopped nuts. Lay onto a cookie sheet lined with wax paper. Repeat with more bananas. Cover with wax paper. Freeze for 4 hours.

Ryan's Energy Bars

3 Tbsp honey, heated until runny
1 cup raw unhulled sesame seeds
1 cup raw sunflower seeds
1/2 cup raisins
1/2 cup chopped nuts
Chopped dried fruits, optional

Combine all ingredients in a large bowl and mix well until thick and coated. Add more honey if necessary but keep the consistency thick. Press into cookie sheets and sit in the fridge overnight. Cut into bars and enjoy. These are a bit sticky but should hold together nicely. (Just don't let the kids have them in the evening!)

> The seeds of the sunflower are rich in protein. Sunflowers can grow as high as 15 feet. There are also dwarf sunflower plants that will only grow 2-3 feet tall, too.
> One sunflower head can produce up to 1,000 seeds!

Perky Pecan Petites
from Carol S., Health Minister[SM]

2 cups raw pecans

1 cup organic raisins

Half an apple, peeled, cored & cut into chunks

Unsweetened, unsulphured, shredded coconut

Alternate pecans, raisins and pieces of apple through Champion or Green Star juicer using the blank. Mix dough to smooth consistency. Take slightly rounded tea-spoonful of dough and roll into ball. Roll in coconut. Dehydrate for 10 hours at 105 degrees. Store in refrigerator. Note: you don't have to dehydrate if you do not wish. It simply makes a better consistency for the cookie.

Carob Icing and Graham Crackers
from Ryan W., 9
from Healthy 4 Him, Recipes for HealThy Living

2 cups cashews, soaked in water 2 hours and drained

1/2 cup carob powder

1/2 cup maple syrup

Blend all in the food processor and spread onto whole wheat organic graham crackers. If too thin add more cashews; if too thick, add more syrup.

Hallelujah Kids

> "India is one of the major producers of cashews. Cashews are valuable as a part of any diet for healthy hearts and cholesterol control."
> *Healthy Nuts* by Gene Spiller, PhD

Banana Ice Cream

Frozen bananas

Run frozen bananas through the Champion or GreenStar juicer with the blank screen in place.

Variations:
Run frozen berries/fruits through in between bananas. Stir in with banana.

Some suggestions:

> **Strawberry**
> **Raspberry**
> **Blueberry**
> **Blackberry**
> **Kiwi**
> **Mango**
> **Pineapple**

Toppings:

> **Chocolate syrup:**
> Mix cocoa powder or carob powder with maple syrup
> **Caramel syrup:**
> Process soaked dates with water for syrup
> **Strawberry syrup:**
> Process fresh strawberries with soaked dates and water or maple syrup
> **Coconut:** unsulphured, unsweetened shredded coconut
> Almonds, chopped
> Walnuts, chopped
> Dates, pitted and chopped

A few more tricks of the trade

Here are some ideas I use to make greens and the less sweet veggies more fun for my 8-year-old son to eat.

Carob Nut Spread for Veggies
This is great to spread on otherwise bland sliced veggies like turnips, radishes, celery root, Jerusalem artichokes. It's also good on celery sticks, carrots, and fruits like apple, pear or banana slices. It can also be used on dehydrated veggie slices/chips, flax crackers, whole grain bread, etc.

Ingredients:

Raw Nut Butter, either homemade or purchased, any kind works. We use almond, tahini (sesame), pumpkin seed, hemp seed or sunflower seed.

Carob Powder, raw or toasted. Use 2-3 teaspoons for every ¿ cup of nut butter.

Distilled Water, to moisten to desired consistency. Start with about the same amount of water as carob powder.

Sweetener isn't really needed but sometimes we use a little bit of Green Stevia Powder to taste since my son is sugar sensitive; but you could use maple sugar, maple syrup, honey, white stevia powder, or any type of sweetener.

This carob spread looks just like chocolate cake frosting but tastes better, and is so much better for us. It adds healthy protein and fats to children's diets and a little goes a long way. If you make it thinner by adding more water, it becomes a dip (carob fondue!) for veggies like broccoli and cauliflower. My son will eat foods he first turned his nose up at if I dress it up with some carob spread.

from Annette K.
Charlottesville, VA

Banana Split
from Victoria L.

1 banana
1 Tbsp almond butter
2 tsp chopped nuts
Coconut

Spread almond butter on banana and roll in chopped nuts. Sprinkle with coconut.

Victoria L.

Hallelujah Baby Food!

> Human breast milk is the perfect food for an infant, and one of the most damaging things a mother can do is to substitute the milk of a cow for her own.
> *The China Study* by Dr. T. Colin Campbell, p. 194

> "…infants or very young children of a certain genetic background, who are weaned from the breast too early onto cow's milk and who, perhaps, become infected with a virus that may corrupt the gut immune system, are likely to have a high risk for Type I Diabetes. Cow's milk consumption by children zero to fourteen years of age in twelve countries shows an almost perfect correlation with Type I Diabetes.
> *The China Study* by Dr. T. Colin Campbell, pp. 189 & 190

He is saying Type ONE diabetes the kind we are told is genetic is not really only genetic "genes do not act in isolation; they need a trigger." We might carry a disease-causing gene but we get the actual disease by triggering it ourselves with what we choose to eat or feed our children!

> A newborn babe is equipped with red corpuscle-making facilities in the bone marrow, which is ready to go to work immediately, but there are at first no gastric juices present to digest solid foods such as protein or starch. Consequently, a baby must have predigested food. Nature (God) amply provides for each stage and condition of life, and here is where the mother eats and digests the food, which is transferred via the blood stream into the mammary glands of the breasts where only the red corpuscles are filtered out - and the infant is actually given an oral blood transfusion by the mother. This is a perfect arrangement, for since the child and mother are of similar flesh and blood, the vibration of the milk is compatible and suitable as a particularized food.
> Dr. John R. Christopher wrote *Herbal Health Care* from which this article was excerpted

> Hypersensitivity to milk is implicated as a cause of sudden death in infancy.
>
> *The Lancet, vol. 2, 7160, November 19, 1960*

> Breastfeeding is known to protect an infant against gastrointestinal pathogens and epidemiological studies indicate that compared to breast-fed infants, formula-fed infants are at a greater risk of dying from sudden infant death syndrome.
>
> *Immunology & Medical Microbiology, 1999*

And still it happens and still we feed our babies man-made formula.

Nursing and pregnant mothers on The Hallelujah Diet® MUST eat an abundance of fresh live foods, cooked vegan dishes, live juices, nuts and seeds to ensure optimal growth and development for their babies! B12 supplementation is also imperative and possibly vitamin D as well.

For easy baby foods, consider simply blending the foods you prepare for the rest of the family from the recipes above, especially smoothies (no honey, salt, spices or peanuts, though).

Pureed foods for the babies should be stored in the refrigerator no longer than two days.

Coconut Milk

When buying young coconuts, pick the heaviest ones. Using a hatchet, whack around the top 3 or 4 times to crack the coconut. Then pry off the top. Scoop out the flesh and blend it in a blender with the water. Option: Squeeze a lime in the coconut milk.

Sweet Almond Milk

> 1/2 cup raw almonds or any other nuts
>
> 3 cups water to cover
>
> 3-5 soaked dates to taste (for making Sweet Almond Milk)

Soak nuts overnight in the refrigerator. Blend in blender with more water and dates to desired consistency. Strain, using cheesecloth. Refrigerate. Use the same or next day.

As China was a nonpastoral society, dairy milks were not part of the normal diet. The Chinese held almond milk in such high esteem that Reay Tannahill, in her Food in History says: "…almond milk had a nutritional reputation and was poured down the throats of privileged infants in astonishing quantities."

From Healthy Nuts by Gene Spiller, PhD

Blended Fruit

All fruits can be peeled then blended with water. Blend only as much as you think Baby will eat. You can always blend more!

Acorn Squash

Cut squash in half, scoop out the seeds and bake cut-side-down in the oven at 350 degrees about 30 minutes until fork-tender. Cool 30 minutes, scoop out flesh and puree in the food processor or blender.

No more meds for this family, now on the Hallelujah Diet

I have 4 children. One was breastfed for 10 months while I was on the Hallelujah Diet. In fact, all of us have been on The Hallelujah Diet for 10 months and have seen amazing results.

Since making the diet change, my daughter has been able to go off all allergy and asthma medication; my son is off all of his dermatology medications and no longer has the upper respiratory problems he used to have.

The baby, who was 20 months old when we started the diet, is incredibly healthy. In fact, he's above all of our other three children for his age and development. Our other three children were raised on the SAD diet.

When we were sick, literally all the time, I cried out to God for help and He answered me in a big way. The Hallelujah Diet was the answer to that prayer!

from Lori
South Carolina

People are amazed that our 1 year old will eat "salad."

Beginning at about 10 - 12 months of age (in addition to breastfeeding) we fed our last two babies:

diced apple
diced pear
mashed bananas
romaine lettuce (the thick, stalk part broken into tiny pieces)
grated carrot
diced celery
blended fruit (apple, pear, banana, blueberries)

I try to keep it simple and have the little ones eat what the rest of us are eating.

from Lisa W.

Sweet Potatoes/Yams

Bake whole sweet potatoes (yellow flesh) or yams (orange flesh) at 350 degrees about 30 minutes until fork-tender. Cool 30 minutes. Peel and puree flesh in the food processor or blender.

Vegetables

Fresh raw vegetables can be blended with water.
Cooked vegetables can be blended with water, almond milk, and/or cooked sweet potato, brown rice or soaked grains.

Orange Avocado

> 1 avocado
> 1-2 oranges, squeezed

Blend the avocado with the fresh-squeezed orange juice in the food processor until light and fluffy. Put the leftovers into a seal-tight plastic bowl for tomorrow or only blend half the avocado and store the other half in a plastic storage bag with the pit in it and blend it with the rest of the orange juice tomorrow.

Broccoli, Rice and Almond Milk

> 1/2 cup brown jasmine rice-soaked overnight in water
>   to cover in the fridge
> 1/2 cup fresh broccoli
> Raw Almond Milk (recipe on page 63)

Drain rice then blend in the food processor with the rest until light and fluffy, adding milk when needed.

Hallelujah Kids

Fruit Plate

Peel and chop pieces of fruit—any kind—one kind at a time or a variety.

Melon Plate

Peel and chop pieces of melon—watermelon, cantaloupe, musk melon, etc.—preferably one variety at a time.

Peaches and Cream

> Peaches, peeled
> Sweet Almond Milk (recipe on page 141)

Blend peaches in food processor and top with Sweet Almond Milk or blend them together. You can add soaked oats for a heavier meal.

Nut milks made from pecans were used by the North American Indians, just like almond, hazelnut, pine nut, walnut and other nut milks were used by the Chinese and Europeans of past centuries. These nut milks were easy to digest for the very young, sick and aging and provided lasting energy for everyone.
From *Healthy Nuts* by Gene Spiller, PhD

Apricot Pudding

> 1-1/3 cup dried unsulphured, unsweetened apricots
> 1 banana
> 1 tsp raw tahini

Cover the apricot with water and soak overnight in the refrigerator. Blend in the food processor or blender with the banana, tahini and soak water until the mixture reaches a pudding-like consistency.

Quinoa Cereal

1 cup quinoa-uncooked
2 cups water
1 apple peeled and shredded
1-2 Tbsp sunflower seeds, chopped (optional)
Maple syrup
Rice or nut milk

Soak and rinse the quinoa in cold water using a fine mesh strainer. Boil quinoa in 2 cups water then simmer 10-15 minutes until water is absorbed. Remove from heat and let cool. Blend in the food processor with remaining ingredients until creamy.

Instead of jarred baby food, spoon-feed fresh avocado to your baby directly from the shell for a nutritious, go-anywhere meal.

Avocados can be mixed with applesauce or cooked squash for variety and nutrition.

Avocados make super after-school snacks. Serve guacamole with baked chips, quesadillas or spread avocado on graham crackers and top with raisins.

From the California Avocado Commission

Messy Mango Pit

Slice a mango into two halves around the large pit. Peel the pit and give it to the baby to suck on (wearing a bib and in a highchair of course!). If you feel like sharing, you could give the baby some pieces of mango flesh too.

Hallelujah Kids

Breast milk and carrot juice start Hallelujah Kids off right...

We feel so blessed to have learned about the Hallelujah Diet before our daughters (age 6 and 3) were born. They both began drinking carrot juice at about 6 months. Our older child had four teeth and was 9 months old and our younger child had two teeth and was 8 months old before I introduced solid foods. We started with fruits then added some avocado and sweet potato. They didn't eat complex carbs until molars came in and that is when I weaned them. My children have never had any formula or cow's milk to drink.

Their diet consists mainly of fruits and vegetables and whole grains. They drink fresh juice and pure water daily.

It is an indescribable blessing to have children who are rarely ill. I cannot be a bigger supporter of a whole foods diet.

Toby and Linda C.
Kentucky

Arien doesn't eat chickens or piggies...

I waited until I was 30 to get pregnant for the first time. I had been on the Hallelujah Diet for almost 2 years at that point-with the exception of some sugar.

I've always been iron anemic and knew that this would probably get worse through my pregnancy. Taking 1-2 tbsp of blackstrap molasses each day kept my iron count up, but also helped me add a few extra pounds!

I had a textbook pregnancy with no issues and my daughter, Arien, was born a very healthy 7 lbs 3 oz and quite alert! She received 9's on both of her APGAR's!

I nursed Arien until she was 20 months old and I was 3 months pregnant
again.

I started trying her out on bananas around 4.5-5 months old. She would also eat avocados occasionally that I blended. I made all of her baby food.

Once she was old enough to chew, she loved steamed broccoli, peas and green beans. She loves bananas, apples, grapes, cherries, plums, peaches, honeydew, watermelon and all of that good stuff!

My husband is not on the Hallelujah Diet but trusts me to do what's right for her. When he's eating chicken, he just tells her this is daddy's chicken, do you eat chickens? She'll tell him no. Same thing with pigs...we saw piglets at a county fair last weekend. I showed her and said, aren't they cute! Do we eat piggies? She told me no.

I do give her a children's multivitamin with B-12 and other B vitamins. Other than that she pretty much eats whole, fresh foods other than the cooked portion at dinner which she rarely likes! I know her patterns might change as she gets older, but it's just like being raised in church. You start them young and that's what they'll remember the most. Arien says, we go to church to praise Jesus! Hopefully when she gets older she'll keep saying, I don't eat chickens or piggies!

from Anita K.

Hallelujah Kids

Organic Farming

Most farmers in this country are what we call "conventional farmers." They rely on synthetic chemicals and fertilizers to grow their crops. These farming chemicals and fertilizers are not found in nature, and they often build up in the environment, polluting our water and soil.

Most of these chemicals remain active for a long time. . . long after their job is done. Although these chemicals can solve many farming problems, some of them are not healthy for the environment or for people.

What's Different about Organic Farmers?

As organic farmers, we grow food differently from conventional farmers because we choose to use nature's ways of solving farming problems. We grow plants without herbicides (weed killers) or fumigants (soil sterilizers). All of our fertilizer (plant food) is natural. Sometimes we do use some insecticides (insect killers) or fungicides (fungus killers), but only special ones that are approved for organic farming. And we use them less often than conventional farmers use chemicals on their crops. Substances approved for organic farming are usually made from natural ingredients and are less harmful to people, animals, and the environment. It takes a little more effort to grow food organically, but it is a good way to grow healthy, strong plants.

Earthbound Farm

Moms, we make up 80 percent of the consumer market in the United States, which means we could be in control of the food industry! We speak with our dollars and right now we are telling the food industry that we don't care if our food is organic or genetically modified or full of sugar and trans fatty acids. We demand; they supply. We are currently demanding boxes of cereals over fresh whole grains. We are demanding beautiful looking fruits and vegetables over organically grown ones which may not be as pretty to look at but a whole better for us and the planet we will leave to our children. Let's rally together and speak loudly with our money telling the food giants we want fresh, natural, organically grown foods and products made from them for our families!

Resources

I suggest you include these resources in your library—perhaps create a lending library with your friends. Be sure to include your kids in the learning process.

"My people are destroyed for lack of knowledge."

Hosea 4:6

Get Healthy! **Stay Balanced**® video series by Hallelujah Acres®. This is the perfect curriculum to take the kids through! If you are a Health Minister℠, please work through the program with your kids. Let them invite friends and their parents too! If you are not a Health Minister℠, find one nearby and sign up for a class with them. A Health Minister℠ is someone trained by Hallelujah Acres® to teach the program. By all means, make the sample recipes that are recommended in the curriculum. Let the kids in on the food prep action too. Kids will be more likely to try something they have made themselves. For you homeschoolers out there, find a Health Minister℠ to give the course at your co-op or for your group.

The Food Show Videos by Hallelujah Acres®.
We watched these as part of the *Get Healthy!*® classes. You can buy these and watch them at your leisure. Most importantly, make the recipes with the kids' help.

Why Christians Get Sick by Rev. Malkmus
Reading this book and looking up the Bible verses that are referenced helped my kids to understand that this diet was not just another fad. You can read this aloud to the younger kids and have the older kids read it themselves.

God's Way to Ultimate Health by Rev. Malkmus
Chapter 5, Where's God in Our Time of Sickness? will help them deal with the sickness that is all around them.

Chapter 7, God's Miraculous Self-Healing Body, presents the concept that is vital to understanding why they need The Hallelujah Diet®.

Let your teen girls read Chapter 13, PMS, Menopause and Diet. Prepare them now for the future that comes all too quickly! Teen girls are suffering from PMS unnecessarily and have the right to know why and how to ease the pain.

Hallelujah Kids

On page 91, you will find The Hallelujah Acres® Healthy Foods Pyramid. The kids can use this to make a neat collage by cutting out pictures and gluing them onto a poster board in the same shape as the pyramid. Hang it on the fridge as a reminder.

Chapter 20, Eliminate Toxins & Disease with a Healthy Colon, is right up kids' alleys. They seem to enjoy talking about eliminating for some strange reason!

When they're done with this book, have them prepare the recipe for Pasta Primavera on page 267. My kids love it.

Recipes for Life by Rhonda Malkmus

This is a great study tool that can be used as a curriculum. One fall, I lead a home economics-type class for homeschool teens using this book. Each week we read through a chapter then made the recipes that best fit with the lesson. For example when we read in Chapter 6 about juicing, we made juices. When we read in Chapter 3 on sodas, we made smoothies. I brought in two blenders and a variety of fresh fruits, rice milk, almond milk and ice cubes and let them make their own creations. It was fun to see what they came up with! One kid put a little bit of everything in his. It looked like mud! But he drank the whole thing and enjoyed it. We even made dehydrated granolas one week and played around with dried fruits and nuts another. They learned how to use a food processor, juicer, blender, knives, cutting board, dehydrator and citrus juicer for making fresh orange juice. You don't need a group of kids to teach a similar class. Just do it in your own kitchen with your own kids or invite some others in to learn with them.

The Food Revolution by John Robbins

My kids and I read through this book together when it came out. Reading this book helped us realize that if we eat the way that promotes the best health for ourselves, we promote the best health for the planet. This book would make a great accompaniment to any Earth Science Curriculum.

Area of Earth's total land mass used as pasture for cattle and other livestock: one-half
John Robbins The Food Revolution, p. 29

Diet for a New America by John Robbins (available in both book and video)

I recommend both even though they are several years old now. The video is not for little kids, however. Its depiction of some of the common practices of factory farming is informative but graphic.

The Truth About Meat and Dairy video by Howard Lyman

I'll always remember the day Corbin watched this video. He said when it was over that he never wanted to eat meat again. This would be a great video for Dad to watch with his sons!

> "One-third of Americans will get cancer and one-quarter will die from it. There are 600 chemical compounds in our bodies that did not even exist 50 years ago."
> Howard Lyman *The Truth About Meat and Dairy*

The China Project by Prof. T. Colin Campbell

A must-read for the teens. Corbin read this last summer at age 12. Reading this would be a great summer science assignment for some extra credit from Mom and Dad. This study will show kids the relationship between eating animal protein and risking cancer and other diseases. The full study is out now in his book titled The China Study which is referenced throughout this book.

> We are leading our youth down a path of disease earlier and earlier in their lives. One third of the young people in this country are over-weight or at risk of becoming overweight. Increasingly, they are falling prey to a form of diabetes that used to be seen only in adults, and these young people now take more prescription drugs than ever before.
> Prof. T. Colin Campbell *The China Study*, p. 3

Eat to Live and *Disease-Proof Your Child* by Dr. Joel Fuhrman, MD

Provide the technical details regarding dietary choices. Teens will be able to read and understand these books.

> Most Americans are not aware that the diet they feed their children guarantees a high cancer probability down the road. They don't' even contemplate that eating fast-food meals may be just as risky (or more so) than letting their children smoke cigarettes.
> Pg. 19 *Eat to Live*

Pregnancy, Children & The Hallelujah Diet by Olin Idol
Recommended for teenage girls and young women as they consider the possibility of motherhood in their future.

Don't Drink Your Milk by Frank Oski, MD
Frank Oski, M.D., head of Pediatric Medicine at John Hopkins University School of Medicine, suggests in his book, *Don't Drink Your Milk!*, that after one to two years of age, the time of "normal" weaning from breastmilk, milk should be removed from the diet completely.

Milk A-Z by Robert Cohen
Kids will run from milk after reading this book! Also, there is a wealth of info available on his web site at www.notmilk.com.

> Dairy products are the leading cause of food allergy, often revealed by constipation, diarrhea and fatigue. Many cases of asthma and sinus infections are reported to be relieved and even eliminated by cutting out dairy.
> Robert Cohen *Milk A-Z*, p. 22

Super Size Me Educationally Enhanced DVD
I recommend this for sixth to twelfth graders. Filmmaker Morgan Spurlock unravels the American obesity epidemic by interviewing experts and subjecting himself to a "McDonalds only" diet for thirty days. The film is as entertaining as it is horrifying as it dives into corporate responsibility, nutritional education, school lunch programs and how we as a nation are eating ourselves to death!

Nutrition and Athletic Performance by Dr. Doug Graham

A good and easy to read book for any young aspiring athlete. A must-have for kids involved in sports.

Your water bill

You know that paper that comes with your water bill once or twice a year that lists the levels of all the stuff in your water? Have the kids look up on the Internet each item that is listed. For example, they will find that arsenic is in the tap water. Ninety percent of industrial arsenic is used as a wood preservative, but it is also found in paints, dyes, metals, drugs, soaps and semi-conductors. Paper production, cement manufacturing, mining and burning fossil fuels also release arsenic into the environment. This information should make anyone think twice about drinking from the fountain or tap!

> "For optimal performance, foods with negative effects must be eliminated from the diet."
> Dr. Doug Graham, *Nutrition and Athletic Performance* pg. 32

Water treatment plant

Get the kids to a field trip at your local water treatment plant to thoroughly gross them out about drinking tap water! Go prepared with questions like, "How much of that gunk over there remains in the water after processing?" and our favorite, "Is that toilet paper floating in that mess?"

Health food stores

This makes another great field trip. Find one that actually sells food then ask for a tour! Ask them to take you through the produce section and explain where it is grown and how you eat it. Find out what has to be peeled, how you peel it, how to pick a good one, when it is in season, etc. Go through the vegan junk food section and read the labels to determine what items you are willing to allow. Buy a few things and let the kids start making new favorites lists. You will also find some packaged vegan junk food that will be good to bring to parties and classrooms for snacks. Just remember to count these items toward their cooked food for the day!

Supplements For Kids

BarleyMax®

BarleyMax® is dehydrated juice from young barley and alfalfa plants providing one of the widest spectrums of naturally occurring nutrients available in a single source.

You can eat it off a spoon, you can mix it in water, you can mix it with carrot juice, you can mix it with Carrot*Juice*Max, you can take it in a capsule, you can put it on your salad...whatever way you like it and even if you don't!

BarleyMax capsules are cool...

I thought of a couple basic things I'd share here that my son didn't bring up. It is understood that he begins the morning with his juice and other liquids (water/herbal tea), then he can have some fresh fruit, then later he can have some more fruit, some trail mix or some muesli. He knows that the juice needs to be taken before he goes on to anything else- this has removed a lot of the power struggle, because the control is in his hands of whether or not he gets something more. We treat it very matter of fact (like you need to get dressed before you can leave the house). The capsules have been a great way to get our son to take BarleyMax- he thinks it's pretty cool being able to swallow caps. When we began him on carrot juice a good trick was to buy a special "juice cup" which was colored so he couldn't see the juice inside!

from Kim W., John's mom

Carrot*Juice*Max

When fresh carrot juice is not available, like when traveling for long periods or on mission trips, Carrot*Juice*Max is a great substitute! Carrot*Juice*Max from Hallelujah Acres® is dried carrot juice. We just bring it along dry then mix in water. We like to mix our dry Carrot*Juice*Max with dry BarleyMax® in a canning jar for packing then spoon it out into a cup and add water when we want it. You can even sprinkle it on popcorn.

B12

> Parents will want to make sure their child's diet includes a regular source of vitamin B12, which is needed for healthy blood and nerve function. Deficiencies are rare, but when they happen, they can be a bit hard to detect. Vitamin B12 is plentiful in many commercial cereals, fortified soy and rice milks, and nutritional yeast. Check the labels for the words cyanocobalamin or B12. Children who do not eat these supplemented products should take a B12 supplement of 3 or more micrograms per day. Spirulina and seaweed are not reliable sources of vitamin B12.
> Physicians Committee for Responsible Medicine

Vitamin D

Vitamin D is produced by our own bodies when our skin is exposed to sunlight at least 15 minutes a day without sunscreen on.

Supplementation may be necessary for those living in northern climates and nursing or pregnant mothers-do this under the supervision of a physician.

> Exposure to sunlight provides most humans with their vitamin D requirement.
> *Journal of Nutrition,* 1996

The darker your skin, the more sun exposure you need. It may take as much as six times more sun exposure to make the same amount of this vitamin in some African Americans as it does Caucasians.

Olin Idol, *Pregnancy, Children & The Hallelujah Diet*, p 22

Give your mother a reason to be glad...

My name is John Wilson. I am 7 years old. I like to play outside with my dog, Lilah. I like doing science experiments. I like to run around the house, wearing a pedometer, so I can get lots of steps. Here's my own favorite recipe: Get some bananas, and some almond butter or tahini and mix it with molasses. Cut up bananas and then dip them into the mix. I eat this in the morning while doing my schoolwork. I also like my mom's soups, carob shakes, and smoothies. I helped make some of the recipes in my mom's cookbooks- I made up the glazed bananas (Everyday Wholesome Eating. . . In the Raw, pg. 169). For lunch I usually have salad or a fruit smoothie. I have been eating healthy for about five years. It's really yummy. My favorite Bible verse is Proverbs 23:25- "Make your father and mother happy. Give your mother a reason to be glad".

from John W., 7

Hallelujah Kids

Recipe Index

Hallelujah Kids

Hallelujah Kids